THE LOCAL MISSION OF HIGHE[R EDUCATI]ON

Principles and Practice

For Newell Fischer,

With thanks & best regards

Edited by
Sjur Bergan, Ira Harkavy, and Ronaldo Munck

GLASNEVIN
PUBLISHING

Published in 2019 by

Glasnevin Publishing
2nd Floor, 13 Upper Baggot Street
Dublin 4, Ireland
www.glasnevinpublishing.com

A Catalogue record for this book can be obtained from the British Library.

Papers used by Glasnevin Publishing are from well managed forests and other responsible sources.

ISBN: 978-1-908689-36-8

CONTENTS

Preface
Professor Brian Mac Craith, President, Dublin City University

Word from the Editors   i
Sjur Bergan, Ira Harkavy, and Ronaldo Munck

SETTING THE SCENE

The Local Mission of Higher Education: a European Challenge   1
Sjur Bergan and Ira Harkavy

What Is an Anchor Institution and Why?   16
David Maurrasse

INSTITUTIONAL PERSPECTIVES

The University and Local Civic Engagement: an Irish Case Study   29
Joanna Ozarowska

Campus and Community Revitalization in the United States: Penn's Evolution
as an Anchor Institution   39
Joann Weeks

Embedding Engagement: the Example of Queen's University Belfast   52
Tony Gallagher

When Your Local Community is Spread Out: the University of the Aegean   63
Spyros Syropoulos

A Traditional University in its Local Community: the Jagiellonian University in
Kraków   74
Stanisław Kistryn

The University of Iceland's Participation in the Local and National Community:
Increasing Impact, Widening Access   80
Steinunn Géstsdóttir

Can International Universities Be Anchor Institutions? Local, Regional, and
Global: the Central European University.   90
Liviu Matei

The Third Mission of Universities: Examples of Good Practice from the Czech
Republic   102
Radka Wildová, Tomáš Fliegel, and Barbora Vokšická

WIDER PERSPECTIVES

The Local Mission of Higher Education: A Global View   115
Pam Fredman

Engagement as Transformative: a south African Example   124
Ahmed Bawa

THE WAY FORWARD   137
Sjur Bergan, Ira Harkavy, and Ronaldo Munck

CONTRIBUTORS   145

PREFACE

The environment in which higher education exists today is very different from the landscape of just a few decades ago. We live in a complex era of political disruption and economic uncertainty. This inevitably brings additional pressures and demands to bear on our universities and higher education institutions.

The current situation only serves to underline the need for higher education to engage purposefully with the broader society in which it operates. Retreating to an ivory tower model is not an option. Dialogue with enterprise and civil society is central to the task of finding sustainable solutions to the challenges we face. This approach has always been central to Dublin City University's mission to 'transform lives and societies through education, research, innovation, and engagement'. I know that many other higher education institutions share these values.

For higher education institutions, the concept and practice of engagement must continually evolve. At DCU we have always been mindful of our impact on our local community and work hard to make our university a model of social inclusion and diversity. Alongside this, we continue to identify new ways of making the university a welcoming space for people with autism, older people and others. DCU recently became Ireland's first 'University of Sanctuary', in recognition of its commitment to welcoming asylum seekers and refugees into the university community and its fostering of a culture of inclusion for all.

In terms of its engagement with government, higher education must be above party politics. However, that is not to say that we should be non-political on matters of democracy, human rights and education. Higher education is vital to a healthy democracy as it entails the democratization of knowledge and fosters healthy political dialogue. By encouraging our students to engage in the democratic process, we create informed citizens who are ready to engage in a positive manner with their communities and society.

I hope that the essays collected in this book - the product of a fascinating workshop organized by the Council of Europe and the Anchor Institutions Task Force held at Dublin City University in 2018 - will provide further impetus for higher education to promote democracy through engagement with the wider society. A European network of Anchor Institutions committed to civic engagement would be a signal contribution at this critical juncture in our history.

Prof. Brian MacCraith
President, Dublin City University

A Word From the Editors

Sjur Bergan, Ira Harkavy, and Ronaldo Munck

The local mission of high education may seem like a contradiction in terms. After all, higher education and research aspires to universality, and they are international by origin, aspiration and – in many cases – current practice. Nevertheless, whatever their real or intended presence on the world stage, higher education institutions are located in specific neighbourhoods and local communities. Some forms of online higher education may be seen as exceptions, but it is worth noting that these are often referred to as "providers" rather than "institutions", and that they are not necessarily subject to the same quality assurance mechanisms as institutions that are part of national higher education systems in Europe or North America.

We contend that higher education institutions are not only located in communities but that they should see themselves as part of those communities. In the United States, higher education institutions are frequently described as "anchored in" their communities because they are unlikely to relocate, hence the term "anchor institutions". A sense of place and location should lead to a sense of belonging and commitment.

This book is an attempt to demonstrate why the local mission of higher education should be given importance as well as to show through examples how this could be done. Commitment must be demonstrated through institutional policy and practice, or it does not exist.

Higher education institutions tend to be significant employers in their region or community and contribute to local economic development through innovation as well as by virtue of students and staff living, buying, and spending in the community. This is important, but we argue in this book that the commitment of higher education institutions to their communities must go beyond the economy and extend to society.

We have explored the democratic mission of higher education elsewhere (Huber and Harkavy (2007); Bergan and Damian (2010); Bergan, Harkavy, and van't Land (2013); Bergan, Gallagher and Harkavy (2015); Bergan and Harkavy (2018); Benson, Harkavy, and Puckett (2007); Benson, Harkavy et al. (2017); Munck 2009 a, 2009 b;

Munck et al. 2012, 2014). Often thought of in voting rights, democracy extends to deliberation and participation, among other areas of life. Higher education should prepare students for democratic deliberation and participation as well as for exercising their rights and – we would argue – obligations as voters.

This book argues that democracy is local as well as national, and that the role of higher education in developing and maintaining local communities that are sustainable politically, socially, environmentally, and economically is crucial. We do not believe that the "ivory tower" is an accurate image of higher education. Had it been, the University would not have survived for centuries as one of our oldest institutions. We do believe, however, that higher education institutions must engage more strongly with their local communities. Many already do but too many do not or do so only insufficiently.

The book grows out of work in both Europe and the United States. The United States is perhaps the precursor in this work, as the Anchors Institutions Task Force (AITF) was set up in 2009 to bring leaders of anchor institutions together at a national level to help them exchange experience and work together for common goals. It now has some 900 members from institutions and communities across the US.

In Europe, the work is inspired by but does not necessarily aim to imitate that of the Anchor Institutions Task Force. On two occasions, the Council of Europe has brought together European higher education leaders to explore the local mission of higher education. The first meeting was held in Rome in June 2017 and the second in Dublin in October 2018. This book builds on the contributions to the second meeting, and we are grateful to Dublin City University for having hosted it. Both meetings served as an eye-opener to some of the participants, who had previously not given much through to their local role.

In the first chapter, Sjur Bergan and Ira Harkavy explore the background for the work on the local mission of higher education and make the case for considering it a European challenge. They link the democratic and local mission of higher education and argue that the global, national, and local roles of higher education institutions are complementary rather than in competition or mutually exclusive. All higher education institutions may not have global ambitions, and some may also not have national aspirations, but all have a local role and should develop policies for it. They can and should do so without in any way being – or being seen as – "parochial". Although the standards of higher education and research are often international, the context in which they are applied, however, is always local as well as national and global.

In the second article, David Maurrasse spells out the "what and why" of the US anchor institutions. Many are higher education institutions, but some are not. They do have in common a commitment to their local community, and that commitment is institutional, through the institutional leaders. Committed faculty and students can do much, but only the leadership can commit and move the whole institution. According to the approach of the Anchor Institutions Task Force (AITF), which Maurrasse directs, institutions of higher education are engaged anchor institution when their entire resources - academic and corporate - are brought together to work with and help improve their local communities.

The main section of the book provides examples of how the local mission can be carried out in practice. This section aims to show that the local mission can be accomplished in numerous ways and in very different circumstances.

Joanna Ozarowska's outlines Dublin City University's local civic engagement as an exemplar of how Ireland has embraced the civic and community engagement mission, not least through its umbrella organisation Campus Engage. Situated in an area of acute social and economic disadvantage DCU has engaged through its teaching and research with the local community to mutual advantage. The 'value' of this engagement can and has been quantified but it also contributes to the less measurable democratisation of society and of knowledge itself. The early strategic orientation towards this mission is now, a decade on, becoming embedded in the routine practices of the university.

Joann Weeks provides an account of how and why the University of Pennsylvania came to be a leading anchor institution. The role of presidential and faculty leadership and efforts to integrate local engagement into the university's academic mission and corporate operations are identified as central to Penn's progress as an engaged university, as is an approach based on democratic partnerships with the community that involve mutual benefit and respect. The contributions of the Netter Center for Community Partnerships, an organization created at Penn to advance local engagement, and economic projects developed by the university's Office of the Executive

Vice President, as well the cooperation between these two offices, are also described as important to Penn's work with its community.

Tony Gallagher's article on Queen's University Belfast describes an institution that now plays a vital role in promoting participation and social inclusion in its community. Diversity was not traditionally valued in Belfast, however, and Queen's has developed from an institution that traditionally served the middle - and upper - class segments of the majority Protestant community to one that aims to serve all social, religious, and ethnic groups in Northern Ireland, *intra et extra muros*, and, not least, that seeks to bring them together.

Spyros Syropoulos describes the University of the Aegean as working in a local community that is "spread out". Serving a vast part of the Greek archipelago, the University of the Aegean was established in 1984 and relates to coal communities on the five islands on which is has campuses as well as in many other islands, as well. The challenges of this geographic diversity is supplemented by those of an environment in which undertaking higher education was an exception rather than a rule. The Aegean example therefore shows, among other things, the importance of higher education being both socially and geographically accessible. As an institution in the south east Mediterranean, on a route that many refugees take from the Middle East, the University of the Aegean sees catering for the higher education needs of refugees as part of its local as well as its global mission.

Stanisław Kistryn describes a prestigious university with a history that goes back centuries: the Jagiellonian University in Kraków. Age, history, prestige, and its comprehensive coverage of academic disciplines could perhaps tempt the Jagiellonian to disregard its local role. Nevertheless, it works with its local and regional community and draws on its strengths as an academically prominent institution. Examples range from an Academic Business Incubator and a Life Science Technology park through work on local government to the protection of biological diversity.

Steinunn Gestsdóttir describes a very different situation. The University of Iceland is not the country's only higher education institution, but it is by far the largest, and it has a near-monopoly on doctoral programmes. Its role is both national and local, and the two may be more difficult to distinguish than in larger countries. Efforts to widen access to higher education, cooperation with economic actors, applied research, public engagement, and student volunteer programmes all focus on the local community; some of the initiatives also have a national scope.

Radka Wildova, Tomáš Fliegl, and Barbora Vokšická describe how what is often referred to as "the third mission" of higher education is carried out at a variety of universities in the Czech Republic. While economic cooperation between institutions and local communities may have been well established, the authors emphasize local engagement in a broader sense, ranging from education initiatives reaching out to populations who have had little access to higher education through initiatives aiming specifically at children, or promoting environment sustainability to activities directed at the homeless or other vulnerable groups, including by providing legal services.

Pam Fredman writes from a global perspective, as President of the International Association of Universities (IAU), but also draws on the experience of her native Sweden, including her home city of Gothenburg. From a policy perspective, Fredman expresses concerns that university rankings, which are given importance in many countries in spite of misgivings about their relevance and methodology, do not include indicators that would give importance to the local mission of higher education. The local mission is multifaceted and raising funding has proved to be a problem. Fredman argues that there should be a "global responsibility of higher education systems but also research funders and other stakeholders to recognize and value the local mission of higher education in terms of academic prestige, funding, and advancement".

Ahmed Bawa looks at the local and democratic mission from a South African perspective. South Africa has seen a disconnect between policy that emphasized engagement and funding criteria that did not. Nevertheless, the tradition of academic activism and engagement that evolved in opposition to as well as in the wake of apartheid has influenced research and development. The recent resurgence of student activism has also been important, and Bawa points to two ways in which this is true: demands for what he terms 'decolonized, quality' education and demands that the chasm between universities and the public be reduced. He concludes that higher education will need to play a key role in educating the citizens of tomorrow and hence to form society.

In the final chapter, we – as editors – seek to outline a way forward. We believe higher education institutions need to be anchored or embedded in their local communities and that knowledge transfer is a two-way process between the higher education institution and the community. We are also emphatic that engaging with the local is fully compatible with global engagement and, indeed, complementary. Dialogue needs to be conducted within and between communities, therefore also in local frameworks. We believe that the further work that will be undertaken, starting with a Council of Europe conference in June 2019, should seek to answer questions such as how we can better embed our higher education institutions within our local communities to build and sustain democracy; whether we can develop a model for local engagement that recognizes the sheer diversity of higher education institutions in terms of size, orientation and mission; and what form of cooperation will best provide a stable European platform for furthering the local mission of higher education and that will eventually bring together in common purpose higher education institutions of varied profiles and ambitions.

Higher education and research are one of the most internationalized areas of human activity, with internationally accepted standards for excellence in research and a high level of interaction and exchange in learning and teaching. Yet, all institutions are situated and belong to a local community. If there ever was a time for higher education institutions to think globally and act locally, that time is now. We hope this book will help both reflection and action.

References

Benson, L., Harkavy, I., &Puckett, J., (2007). *Dewey's Dream: Universities and Democracies in an Age of Democratic Reform.* Philadelphia, PA: Temple University Press

Benson, L., Harkavy, I., Puckett, J., Hartley, M., Hodges, R., Johnston, F. & Weeks, J.(2017): *Knowledge for Social Change: Bacon, Dewey, and the Revolutionary Transformation of Research Universities in the Twenty-First Century.* Philadelphia, PA: Temple University Press

Bergan, Sjur and Radu Damian (eds.) (2010): *Higher Education for Modern Societies: Competences and Values* Strasbourg: Council of Europe Publishing. Council of Europe Higher Education Series No. 15

Bergan, Sjur; Tony Gallagher, and Ira Harkavy (eds.) (2015): *Higher Education for Democratic Innovation* Strasbourg: Council of Europe Publishing. Council of Europe Higher Education Series No. 21

Bergan, Sjur and Ira Harkavy (eds.) (2018): *Higher Education for Diversity, Social Inclusion and Community. A Democratic Imperative* Strasbourg: Council of Europe Publishing. Council of Europe Higher Education Series No. 22

Bergan, Sjur; Ira Harkavy and Hilligje van't Land (eds.) (2013): *Reimagining Democratic Societies: a New Era of Personal and Social Responsibility* Strasbourg: Council of Europe Publishing. Council of Europe Higher Education Series No. 18

Huber, Josef and Ira Harkavy (eds.) (2007): *Higher Education and Democratic Culture: Citizenship, Human Rights and Civic Responsibility* Strasbourg: Council of Europe Publishing – Council of Europe Higher Education Series No. 8

Munck, R (2009 a) Bridging the 'Town and Gown' Divide' (with D. O'Broin) in A. Mc Crann (ed) *Memories, Milestones and New Horizons: Reflection on the Regeneration of Ballymun.* Belfast: Blackstaff Press

Munck, R (2009 b) *Civic Engagement in Irish Universities: Creating Global Citizens'* Arts and Humanities in Higher Education, Vol. 8 No 4

Munck, R, L.Mc Ilrath, A Lyons (eds.) (2012) *Higher Education and Civic Engagement: Comparative Perspectives* New York: Palgrave

Munck, R, L Mc Ilrath, B. Hall and R.Tandon (eds.) (2014) *Higher Education and Community Based Research: Towards a New Paradigm* (contributing lead editor) New York: Palgrave Macmillan

SETTING THE SCENE

CHAPTER 1
THE LOCAL MISSION OF HIGHER EDUCATION: A EUROPEAN CHALLENGE

Sjur Bergan and Ira Harkavy

Context

On both sides of the Atlantic there is broad concern that democracy is challenged. While democracy is mediated through institutions and laws that to some extent vary between countries and traditions, democracy appeared to be an idea whose broad features were the subject of consent and even enthusiasm from Hawaii to Helsinki and from Georgia to Gaziantep.

Developments since the 2008 financial crisis have challenged the belief that democracy is a common aspiration. The beginnings of what might be termed the democratic crisis, while impossible to pinpoint with any pretension of exactitude, might be plausibly dated as September 11, 2001. More specifically, it might be argued that insecurity following from terrorist attacks along with deep economic insecurity, and a related perception that the wealthy were relatively untouched by (and even benefitted from) the financial crisis, led to disillusion with democratic institutions and democracy itself. It would, moreover, seem difficult to argue that actions taken by governments committed to democracy were largely effective in decreasing these insecurities.

September 11 was neither the first nor the last terrorist attack but no other attack has had such an impact. It seems to have signalled the end of an era and the start of new, tougher, more polarized times, with increasing occurrence of hate speech – not least on social media. It also resulted in increased acceptance of what would previously have been considered outrageous statements, as well as increased public acceptance of measures intended to improve public security but that also reduce personal liberty. One example is the security measures surrounding the Christmas market in Strasbourg, the city of residence of one of the authors of this article. Strasbourg residents generally consider these measures cumbersome but justified even if they could be seen as limiting freedom of movement. Tragically, they did not, however, prevent a terrorist attack on the Strasbourg Christmas market on December 11, 2018 that left 5 dead and several victims wounded.

The 2008 financial crisis was also not the first, and it certainly will not be the last. We should not forget that some citizens on both sides of the Atlantic live in a seemingly endless financial crisis, even within societies that are reasonably affluent. However, the 2008 crisis heightened a feeling of insecurity that had already been aroused, reinforcing fear, and the search for easy solutions across the globe. Many people seem to want to establish clear borders in an age where at least some traditional borders and boundaries seemed destined to disappear. In Europe, for example, the Schengen Agreement abolishing passport controls between participating countries comes under periods of attacks, above all from nationalist politicians.

Whatever the origin, the current political climate is characterized by distrust, confrontation and the absence of dialogue. A view of politics and governance as arenas of negotiations, compromise and "the art of the possible" increasingly seems to cede to a view of politics as a game of "the winner takes all," where governance as less important. There is distrust of institutions and of established parties. As we write these lines, widespread protests in France known as Yellow Vests (*gilets jaunes*) are an example. Starting as a protest against an increase in the tax on gas, the protests quickly took on a much broader anti-establishment agenda. They constitute a series of grass roots initiatives organized in large part through social media and with few identifiable national leaders. Protesters are divided on whether to seek a broader political role, e.g. by running for election against established parties. For some protesters, this would be a logical step to take, whereas for others this would betray the anti-establishment origin of the protest movement and its scepticism of established parties.

Beyond distrust of parties and institutions, however, the very notions of facts and expertise are questioned. Terms like "alternative facts" and "fake news" are not necessarily seen as contradictions in terms. At least in Europe, this mix translates into support for populist parties, which are often of the far right but in some cases also of the far left, and "illiberal democracy" has been added to a list of terms that are contradictory by nature but increasingly used without quotation marks. In the United States and Europe, these terms have been used to attack science, knowledge, and democracy itself.

Higher Education and Democracy

It is our contention that higher education has a key role to play in upholding and developing democracy, which includes a commitment to human rights as well as to intercultural dialogue. The Council of Europe and the International Consortium for Higher Education, Civic Responsibility and Democracy have a long standing commitment to the democratic mission of higher education, as demonstrated through a series of Global Fora and publications (Huber and Harkavy (2007), Bergan and Damian (2010), Bergan, Harkavy, and van't Land (2013), Bergan, Gallagher and Harkavy (2015), Bergan and Harkavy (2018)).

The Council of Europe has also developed an understanding of education that goes beyond the traditional emphasis on preparation for the labour market, not by claiming that this purpose is unimportant but by seeing it as one of several purposes of education. Thus, the Council of Europe sees four major purposes of higher education and, by extension, of all strands of education:

> ➢ preparation for sustainable employment;
> ➢ preparation for life as active citizens in democratic societies;
> ➢ personal development;
> ➢ the development and maintenance, through teaching, learning and research, of a broad, advanced knowledge base (Bergan 2005, Council of Europe 2007).

While the degree of academic specialization is more advanced at higher than at secondary education level, all stands and levels of education – including higher education – should develop transversal as well as subject specific competences. The latter are perhaps immediately comprehensible and designate e.g. what chemists or historians should know, understand, and be able to do within their chosen academic discipline. Transversal competences are those any higher education graduate at a given level should have, regardless of academic discipline. In Europe, the concept of transversal and subject specific competences was developed in particular within the TUNING project (González and Wagenaar 2005).

While what a student knows, understands, and is able to do is the traditional definition of learning outcomes, there is good reason to contend that an essential element is missing from this understanding: the ethical dimension. We may be able to do something that we should, for ethical, or other reasons, abstain from doing. Our understanding of learning outcomes is therefore broader: it is what a student knows, understands, is able to do and also is willing to do (or refrain from doing). This understanding of learning outcomes is at the root of the Council of Europe's Reference Framework of Competences for Democratic Culture (Council of Europe 2018), and it is also essential to the role of higher education in promoting democracy and human rights.

Types and Missions of Higher Education Institutions

Quality is a universally acknowledged aspiration for higher education institutions, and for that matter for any part of the education system. No Minister of Education or institutional leader can afford to admit aiming for second best. The increasing prominence of rankings and "excellence initiatives" further drive the quest for quality.

What is in itself a laudable quest, however, suffers from lack of clarity about what is meant by quality. Rankings largely measure research performance, some in a limited number of academic disciplines, mostly natural sciences, and say little of value about the overall quality of an institution or its learning environment (Bergan 2011, Rauhvargers 2011, 2013).

There is also a case for considering the quality of individual institutions separately from the quality of education systems. While different higher education institutions will necessarily have different selection criteria, an education system cannot be considered of high quality unless it provides opportunities for all learners commensurate with their potential and aspirations (Council of Europe 2012). Moreover, each institution benefits from a diverse student body that brings a range of experiences, perspectives, skills and backgrounds to the learning environment.

Higher education institutions are diverse in size, location, governance arrangements, budgets, ownership, and many other factors. This diversity also extends their academic profile, ambitions, and views of their own mission. Whereas some aspire to be world class research and teaching institutions in a broad range of academic disciplines, others aspire to research excellence in a relatively narrow range of disciplines, to research-based excellence in teaching at all levels, to excellence in teaching at first degree/Bachelor level, or they may have a number of other aspirations. As societies, we need higher education to fulfil all of these roles, and several more. All are legitimate, and all can be fulfilled more or less well.

It would, however, be unfair and counter-productive to assess all higher education institutions according to the same criteria without taking account of their stated mission and aspirations. Just as a marathon runner should not be assessed on the basis of her results throwing the javelin, an institution that defines its role primarily in relation to teaching should not be judged according to the same criteria as one with world class research ambitions.

Higher education institutions, then, can define their mission(s) in relation to one or more of a set of possible roles and aspirations. It is important that they state their mission(s), otherwise they can neither develop it nor be assessed on the basis of it. Public authorities as well as other funders may have views on whether the missions as defined by any given institutions are legitimate and pertinent, and they may adjust their funding of the institution accordingly. They cannot, however, easily challenge the quality of an institution by referring to other missions and ambitions than the ones the institution has defined for itself.

Most institutions would have more than one stated mission. As demonstrated by the University of Pennsylvania (Weeks, this volume), it is perfectly possible, indeed appropriate and beneficial, to combine missions and aspirations as a world class research and teaching institutions with a mission of working with and improving the local community. In fact, for Penn, as well as other higher education institutions, local engagement is a means for advancing research, teaching, and learning, as well as service. Queen's University Belfast is one of several European examples (Gallagher and Harrison 2015, McDonald et al. 2015).

Other institutions have different missions. In Finland, Åbo Akademi provides higher education in Swedish primarily for Finland's Swedish language minority, even if native Finnish speakers and other students with sufficient proficiency in Swedish are welcome. It does not compromise on academic quality, but it has other missions in addition to high quality teaching and research. Åbo Akademi interacts with a broader Swedish language and international academic community outside of Finland and describes itself as an "internationally acknowledged research university with a unique role as the bridge between the university communities in Finland and the other Nordic countries". This goal is made more realizable since most educated native speakers of Swedish in Finland are also highly proficient in Finnish. Åbo Akademi is essential to the Swedish speaking community in Finland, and its education quality has enabled it to continue to play this role.

In the United States, community colleges typically provide entry level higher education for students that could be unsure about their academic aspirations, have insufficient means to study at colleges and universities, need to combine work and study, and/or might not qualify for admission to more academically demanding institutions. Community colleges fulfil a very important mission of social inclusion and of providing higher education opportunities for many who would otherwise not have qualified (Murphy 2013, 2018; Padrón 2013). They cannot fulfil their mission without providing teaching and learning of acceptable quality but it would be unreasonable to judge them on the same criteria as e.g., the University of Pennsylvania. If a community college provided programmes that were not adapted to their students, they would not be providing quality education for this group. Realizing their mission, moreover, is crucial for a developing and sustaining a diverse, inclusive democratic society.

This reminds us of the good but essentially unanswerable question: which is the best university? Is it the one that helps well qualified secondary school graduates achieve academic excellence or the one that helps those who barely graduated from secondary schools – or perhaps did not – achieve reasonable higher education competences? Or is it one devoted to advancing research across a range of disciplines or one that has a more narrow research focus in the sciences for example? Quality, simply put, cannot be assessed without reference to purpose.

Higher Education Institutions as Local Actors
The United States is a country of more than 300 million inhabitants and over 4,500 higher education institutions. Countries like Germany, Russia the United Kingdom each have from almost 200 to over 800 higher education institutions of different sizes, profiles, and aspirations. Smaller European countries naturally have far fewer institutions, and the smallest countries have only one or two. Andorra, Liechtenstein, and Malta would be examples. In these cases, there may be no clear distinction between the national and local role of an institution. In many of the smaller and medium sized countries, even

where there are a number of institutions, one or two institutions have historically played a national rather than local or regional role.

Democracy can also be thought of as a national rather than local issue. There is considerable truth to this, as political systems and laws are national. It is exceedingly difficult to exercise democracy at local level if the national political system is authoritarian. Within democratic systems, however, democracy is local and regional as well as national. Democratic institutions comprise municipal councils as well as national parliaments, elections are held to representative bodies at local and regional as well as national level, and democratic participation is most easily carried out locally.

Democracy is, of course, much more than politics or a political system. It is, as the educator and philosopher John Dewey wrote "a way of life," encompassing all aspects of society, including the economic, social, cultural and political systems. (Dewey 1993: 241). Democratic culture, a concept central to the ongoing partnership and cooperative work between the Council of Europe and the International Consortium for Higher Educations, Civic Responsibility and Democracy, captures this robust concept of democracy. It also captures the notion that "Democracy is not just a voting system. It is a culture that respects truth," (Jason Stanley, quoted in Kingsley 2018). Dewey also emphasized that democracy has to be built on face-to-face interactions in which human beings work together cooperatively to solve the ongoing problems of life. Or, as Dewey wrote in 1927, "Democracy must begin at home, and its home is the neighborly community." (Boydston 1981: 368)

For higher education institutions to effectively and optimally contribute to democracy, they, therefore, need to see themselves as being not only in but also of their local communities. Regardless of what other missions they may see for themselves, higher education institutions need to connect democratically and in mutually beneficial ways to their local communities. Of course, some - perhaps more than some - higher education institutions do, but it is worth examining possible roles in more detail.

Higher education institutions are important economic actors in their communities. They might well be the largest local employer, and students may contribute very substantially to the local economy through rent and purchases. They are catalysts and hubs for local and regional economies not only as employers, but also as real estate developers, clients for area vendors, and incubators for business and technology. In cities that have experienced a decrease in capital investments and the departure of industrial jobs, institutions of higher learning often serve as critical sources of employment and stability. In addition, they frequently educate many of those who will later work in the city or region in different capacities, and they engage in the local economy through science parks, innovation schemes, and cooperation with local companies.

Our concern is, however, with a broader understanding of the role of higher education institutions in their communities. In some cases, an institution is so central to the community that we talk of "university cities", which would indicate a close relationship; Oxford and Cambridge in the United Kingdom, Coimbra in Portugal, and Salamanca in Spain would be typical examples. At the same time, however, we also speak about "town and gown", which would indicate that the relationship might be far less than symbiotic.

If we move from considering an economic to a societal role, higher education institutions have several options. They require commitment and engagement from the institutions and their leadership as well as from students, faculty, and staff. They also require commitment from the local community. In cases where the relationship has been distant or even antagonistic for a long time, determined leaders both at the institutions and in the local community can turn this around if they work together. A telling example is Widener University in Chester, Pennsylvania when James T. Harris served as president (Harris and Pickron-Davis 2015). Widener, whose origins lie in a military college, had a long history of keeping aloof from the city. Chester, for its part, was a thriving industrial city largely centred on its shipyard. When the industry declined, so did the city, to the point of being described as a "failed city" with severe problems of crime – often drug related – as well as a public school system that was among the worst performers in Pennsylvania. Mutual scepticism, even hostility, between the university and city leadership could be overcome only gradually and only through determined democratic efforts by a new university president in the early 2000's. The university developed a community service strategy and consulting local authorities as well as civil society was important to its gradual success. This work also laid basis for closer cooperation between "town and gown" when Chester was hit by a crime wave in the wake of the 2008 recession.

The example of Widener and Chester illustrates several roles a higher education institution can play in its local community. Education is an obvious, perhaps the primary, one for a university. Local schools may struggle in more ways than one, and a university might not be able to address all of the issues, for example if lack of funding is an important part of the problem. But it can educate teachers through both initial and in-service training, and it can work more directly with schools to help improve academic achievements and services. It can also provide local schools with access to of its premises, ranging from sports grounds to laboratories.

Not least, higher education institutions can encourage their students to work with their local communities, in particular with local schools. University professors may be good teachers, but they are not necessarily accessible role models for children and young people from challenging environments; nor are many university teachers perhaps very good at teaching primary and secondary school students. Higher education students, however, are a different story. They are not much older than the children and young people with whom they will be working, and some of them might come from similar backgrounds. Higher education institutions can also engage students in academic partnerships through service learning, community-based participatory research, and democratic implementation research, which are designed to improve the school and the community, as well as research, teaching, learning and service at the university (Benson, Harkavy et al. 2017). By the weight of their own examples, higher education institutions not only can teach or help with homework, they can also provide inspiration and motivation. Queen's University Belfast went from an institution that people in the Sandy Row community walked past frequently, but in which they never set foot, to working with local youth in a community centre to give them the motivation to aspire to higher education as well as the competences to make this aspiration realistic (McDonald et al. 2015).

Higher education institutions may also work with civil society in other ways and encourage their students to do so. Faculty and staff can offer counselling in their area of expertise; the long-standing counselling service offered by law students at the University of Oslo is but one example. They may help with the integration of immigrants and refugees, as in the examples of LUMSA university in Rome (Agrusti 2018) or Augsburg University in Minneapolis (Pribbenow

2018) or through the many initiatives includes in the European University Association's Refugees Welcome Map.

Institutions can promote student engagement with the local community by facilitating contacts and by creating an environment in which such engagement is "the normal thing to do". They may also make community outreach an important part of their institutional policies and award study credits for students who engage, whether through voluntary work or as part of their study programme. In a European context, the reform of qualifications framework and study programmes through the European Higher Education Area as well as the widespread introduction of ECTS credits demonstrate how structural reforms can serve a wider purpose.

Anchor Institutions

In the United States, "anchor institutions" designate institutions that are pillars of their local society through their community engagement work (Guarasci and Maurrasse 2015, Maurrasse this volume). The term "anchor" arises from the fact that they are anchored in their community – these institutions will not easily be uprooted from their communities and move elsewhere. Many but not all anchor institutions are universities; some are medical centers, hospitals, schools, museums, art institutions, community foundations, libraries, or other institutions of importance to their community, including certain businesses. Anchor institutions when they function as genuine partners with their communities emphasize "social responsibility, including values of collaboration and partnership, equity and social justice, democracy and democratic practice, and commitment to place and community" (Guarasci and Maurrasse 2015: 102).

The Anchors Institutions Task Force (AITF) brings leaders of anchor institutions together at a national level in the US to help them exchange experience and work together for common goals. Established in 2009, the AITF has some 900 members from institutions and communities across the US, with its annual conferences as a centrepiece of its activities.

The Local Mission – a European Issue?

It may sound ironic to ask whether the local mission should not be a European concern, but as the experience of the AITF shows, exchanging experience and working together is of paramount importance. This has been recognized at both national and international level. Many countries have national associations of local authorities, and the Council of Europe has both a Congress of Local and Regional Authorities and an Intercultural Cities Programme.

We therefore believe there would considerable advantages in bringing together European higher education institutions that see engaging with the local community as part of their mission. Like the AITF in the US, this would ideally bring together institutions of quite different backgrounds and profiles.

This work could be inspired by and cooperate with, but should not copy, the AITF. And the work has in fact begun. In June 2017, the Council of Europe and the AITF brought together some 20 European higher education leaders in Rome, on the eve of the Global Forum on "Higher Education for Diversity, Social Inclusion and Community: a Democratic Imperative" (Bergan and Harkavy 2018), for a first exploration of the local mission of higher education. To some of those present, this meeting was an eye-opener, in that they had previously not reflected on their local role, even if they play one, in addition to their national and international mission.

A second meeting was held at Dublin City University in October 2018, and this book is one of the results. The book shows the variety of experiences that were shared and explores some possible ways forward. A third meeting will be organized in Strasbourg in June 2019, on the eve of another Global Forum, this time focusing on "Academic Freedom, Institutional Autonomy, and the Future of Democracy". We hope that at this meeting a first step towards organized European cooperation may be taken.

Such cooperation could take one of several forms. One could think of a network. Even if some participants at the Dublin meeting felt that there are already too many university networks in Europe, and that institutional leaders find it difficult to relate to them, the majority of participants clearly supported the idea. A task force may be another option, and we would need to define its precise remit and composition. We could also start off with a series of regular meetings with some commitments from institutions to participate regularly. Regardless of the form, it will be important that the cooperation benefit from the commitment and preferably also participation of institutional leaders.

We aim to start at a relatively modest scale and add only a few institutions to those that participated in one or both previous meetings.

The goal will be to establish a form of cooperation that will provide a stable European platform for furthering the local mission of higher education and that will eventually gather institutions of different profiles and ambitions, with commitment by institutional leaders, and comprising institutions from a majority of the 50 States party to the European Cultural Convention, representing all parts of the continent. They should both benefit from and contribute to the sharing of experiences within the AITF and fora in other parts of the world.

This takes us back to our starting point for this chapter: democracy is under stronger pressure today than it was a decade ago. While democratic institutions, laws, and elections are essential, they will not function unless they are rooted in a culture of democracy: a set of attitudes and behaviours that value diversity of opinion and experience, that combines a commitment to majority rule with a commitment to minority rights, and that hold that conflicts should be resolved through peaceful dialogue rather than use of force.

A culture of democracy can only be built through education, at all levels from pre-primary to higher education. A culture of democracy is not like skiing or riding a bike; an ability that once acquired is rarely lost even if it can improve with practice. Rather, a culture of democracy is like a language: if you do not practice it, you will eventually lose it. That is true of foreign languages, it is true of one's native language, and it is true of the culture of democracy. Higher education carries an important responsibility for the future of our democracies. Higher education cannot exercise this responsibility successfully without engaging in its local community as well as nationally and internationally. Community engagement cannot be optional for higher education institutions, and we need to pool our experience and join forces to develop good policies and practice, at a European as well as a global level.

References

Agrusti, Gabriella (2018): "Refugees in European Higher Education – Complex pathways in Diversity", in Bergan, Sjur and Ira Harkavy (eds.) (2018): *Higher Education for Diversity, Social Inclusion and Community. A Democratic Imperative* Strasbourg: Council of Europe Publishing. Council of Europe Higher Education Series No. 22, pp. 117 – 129

Benson, Lee, Harkavy, Ira, Hartley, Matthew, Hodges, Rita A., Johnston, Francis. E., Puckett, John, and Weeks, Joann (2017): *Knowledge for Social Change: Bacon, Dewey, and the Revolutionary Transformation of Research Universities in the Twenty-First Century*. Philadelphia: Temple University Press.

Bergan, Sjur (2005): "Higher Education as a "Public Good and a Public Responsibility": What Does it Mean?", in Luc Weber and Sjur Bergan (eds.): *The Public Responsibility for Higher Education and Research* (Strasbourg 2005: Council of Europe Publishing –Council of Europe Higher Education Series No. 2), pp. 13 – 28

Bergan, Sjur (2010): "Reflections on Ranking in Europe", in *Not by Bread Alone* (Strasbourg: Council of Europe Publishing. Council of Europe Higher Education Series No. 17), pp. 159 - 174

Bergan, Sjur and Radu Damian (eds.) (2010): *Higher Education for Modern Societies: Competences and Values* Strasbourg: Council of Europe Publishing. Council of Europe Higher Education Series No. 15

Bergan, Sjur; Tony Gallagher, and Ira Harkavy (eds.) (2015): *Higher Education for Democratic Innovation* Strasbourg: Council of Europe Publishing. Council of Europe Higher Education Series No. 21

Bergan, Sjur and Ira Harkavy (eds.) (2018): *Higher Education for Diversity, Social Inclusion and Community. A Democratic Imperative* Strasbourg: Council of Europe Publishing. Council of Europe Higher Education Series No. 22

Bergan, Sjur; Ira Harkavy and Hilligje van't Land (eds.) (2013): *Reimagining Democratic Societies: a New Era of Personal and Social Responsibility* Strasbourg: Council of Europe Publishing. Council of Europe Higher Education Series No. 18

Boydston Jo Ann (ed.) (1981): *The Later Works of John Dewey, 1925–1953, vol. 2.* Carbondale: Southern Illinois University; digitally reproduced in Larry Hickman, L. (ed.) (1996): The Collected Works of John Dewey, 1882–1953: The Electronic Edition. Charlottesville, VA: InteLex Corporation.

Council of Europe (2007): Recommendation CM/Rec(2007)6 of the Committee of Ministers to member states on the public responsibility for higher education and research

Council of Europe (2012): Recommendation CM/Rec(2012)13 of the Committee of Ministers to member States on ensuring quality education

Council of Europe (2018): Reference Framework of Competences for Democratic Culture. Volume 1: Context, concepts, and model Volume 2: Descriptors Volume 3: Guidance for Implementation Strasbourg: Council of Europe Publishing

Dewey, John (1939): "Creative Democracy: The Task Before Us" in Morris, D. and Shapiro, I. (ed.) (1993): *The Political Writings*. Indianapolis/Cambridge: Hackett Publishing Company, pp. 240-245

Gallagher, Tony and Jennifer Harrison (2015): "Civic Engagement in a Divided Society: the Role of Queen's University Belfast in Northern Ireland", in Sjur Bergan, Tony Gallagher, and Ira Harkavy (eds.): *Higher Education for Democratic Innovation* Strasbourg: Council of Europe Publishing. Council of Europe Higher Education Series No. 21, pp. 51 - 62

González, J. and Wagenaar, R. (2005): Tuning Educational Structures in Europe. Universities' Contribution to the Bologna Process. Final Report Pilot Project Phase 2. Publicaciones de la Universidad de Deusto, Bilbao and Groningen

Guarasci, Richard and David Maurrasse (2015): "Higher Education Institutions as Pillars of Their Communities – the Role of Anchor Institutions", in Sjur Bergan, Tony Gallagher, and Ira Harkavy (eds.): *Higher Education for Democratic Innovation* Strasbourg: Council of Europe Publishing. Council of Europe Higher Education Series No. 21, pp. 101 - 108

Harris, James T. and Marcine Pickron-Davis (2015): "Case Study of Widener University: a Story about Conflict and Collaboration", in Bergan, Sjur; Tony Gallagher, and Ira Harkavy (eds.) (2015): *Higher Education for Democratic Innovation* Strasbourg: Council of Europe Publishing. Council of Europe Higher Education Series No. 21, pp. 71 - 83

Huber, Josef and Ira Harkavy (eds.) (2007): *Higher Education and Democratic Culture: Citizenship, Human Rights and Civic Responsibility* Strasbourg: Council of Europe Publishing – Council of Europe Higher Education Series No. 8

Kingsley, Patrick (2018): "On the Surface, Hungary Is a Democracy. But What Lies Underneath?" in The New York Times, online edition, December 25, 2018, available at https://www.nytimes.com/2018/12/25/world/europe/hungary-democracy-orban.html, accessed January 4, 2019.

Maurrasse, David (this volume): "What is an Anchor Institution and Why?"

McDonald, Jackie, Nikki Johnston and Garnet "Buzz" Busby with Tony Gallagher: "Community engagement in Belfast: Queen's University and the Sandy Row community", in Sjur Bergan, Tony Gallagher, and Ira Harkavy (eds.): *Higher Education for Democratic Innovation* Strasbourg: Council of Europe Publishing. Council of Europe Higher Education Series No. 21, pp. 63 – 69

Murphy, Brian (2013): ""Democracy at De Anza College", in Sjur Bergan, Ira Harkavy and Hilligje van't Land (eds.): *Reimagining Democratic Societies: a New Era of Personal and Social Responsibility* Strasbourg: Council of Europe Publishing. Council of Europe Higher Education Series No. 18, pp. 219 - 227

Murphy, Brian (2018): "Refugees, Immigrants, and Migrants in Higher Education – The Perspective of an Open Access Institution", in Sjur Bergan and Ira Harkavy (eds.): *Higher Education for Diversity, Social Inclusion and Community. A Democratic Imperative* Strasbourg: Council of Europe Publishing. Council of Europe Higher Education Series No. 22, pp. 131 – 141

Padrón, Eduardo J. (2013): "Reimagining Democratic Societies: a New Era of Personal and Social Responsibility", in Sjur Bergan, Ira Harkavy and Hilligje van't Land (eds*.): Reimagining Democratic Societies: a New Era of Personal and Social Responsibility* Strasbourg: Council of Europe Publishing. Council of Europe Higher Education Series No. 18, pp. 55 – 61

Pribbenow, Paul C. (2018): "Hospitality is not enough – Reflections on Universities and the Immigrant Experience", in Bergan, Sjur and Ira Harkavy (eds.) (2018): *Higher Education for Diversity, Social Inclusion and Community. A Democratic Imperative* Strasbourg: Council of Europe Publishing. Council of Europe Higher Education Series No. 22, pp. 143 - 150

Rauhvargers, Andrejs (2011), Global university rankings and their impact, European University Association, Brussels.

Rauhvargers, Andrejs (2013), Global university rankings and their impact – Report II, European University Association, Brussels.

Weeks, Joann (this volume): "Campus and Community Revitalisation: Penn's Evolution as an Anchor Institution"

CHAPTER 2
WHAT IS AN ANCHOR INSTITUTION AND WHY?

David Maurrasse

Context of the Contemporary Anchor Institutions Movement
In recent years, a movement to encourage enduring organizations that remain in their local communities to deepen their local engagement has been evolving and growing. The Anchor Institutions Task Force (AITF)[1] has built a US based network of over 900 leaders of anchor institutions and other partners who are promoting the role of anchor institutions in community and economic development. The AITF has been organizing individuals in anchor institutions from various fields and representatives[2] of a range of other organizations to exchange ideas to determine the best possible ways in which anchor institutions can contribute to equitable growth and expanded opportunities for vulnerable populations in neighbourhoods, cities, and regions. AITF is values-oriented, suggesting that anchor institutions' involvement in their communities should be guided by a commitment to democracy and democratic practice, collaboration, social justice and equity, and a commitment to place.

The contemporary anchor institutions movement began with an emphasis largely on institutions of higher education. The notion of "anchor" suggests stability in place – organizations that do not tend to relocate from their geographical surroundings. As economies and demographics have shifted over recent years, institutions of higher education have tended to remain in their communities, even in instances of substantial capital flight. As the anchor institutions movement has grown, many other types of institutions have been

---

[1] www.margainc.com/initiatives/aitf/ (accessed, January 22, 2019)
[2] Representatives in AITF tend to be senior executives at anchor institutions, including Chief Executive Officers/Presidents/Chancellors and numerous Vice Presidents, who are often responsible for external affairs and community and economic development in their job responsibilities. The anchor institutions include numerous associations as well as supportive organizations serving the field (i.e. consultants and researchers). Executives/principals of these organizations are among members as well. Programme staff at government agencies, executives and programme staff at philanthropic institutions are also among representatives in AITF's membership.

identified as stable forms of capital in their communities, including hospitals, libraries, arts and cultural institutions, and many other types of organizations that tend to remain in their surroundings.

Uncertainty has been a reality facing many populations around the world. In the face of such instability, there is a desire to find entities that are consistent, which can be sources of knowledge, resources, employment, and various forms of capital. As the nature of government changes, increasingly local leaders, policymakers and others are seeking partners that can bring expertise and resources towards addressing some of the most pressing issues of our times. Many governments lack the resources to adequately address widespread poverty, inequality in education, disparities in health care, climate change, and any range of other matter. Our times[3] have made it clear that collaboration across sectors is required to improve communities. Anchor institutions represent important local assets that can be harnessed through partnerships to improve localities. Increasingly, it is difficult to imagine demonstrable equitable improvements in communities without the active participation of anchor institutions in directly addressing the challenges confronting many local communities.

The idea of anchor institutions is not entirely new (CEOs for Cities 2010, Dragicevic 2105, Dubb and Howard 2102, Maurrasse 2007, Harkavy et al. 2009, Rivlin and O'Cleireacain 2001). Following the industrial revolution, manufacturing firms became the bedrock of many local communities. They were the most significant local

---

[3] With limited government resources to, for example, strengthen overcrowded public schools, there is a need for other actors to play a role in addressing such a challenge. This is characteristic of contemporary times. Many nonprofit anchor institutions, such as universities and hospitals, have been asked to pay additional funds to their municipal governments (Payments in Lieu of Taxes) in order to account for their tax-free status. This is another tendency that is characteristic of the increased need at the local level for additional resources to be applied to meeting public needs. Additionally, the nature of the contemporary economy, which is fluid and knowledge-oriented, can create insecurity in localities. Capital flight is common in communities. Large corporations (as was very evident in Amazon's deal with New York City) seek substantial tax breaks in order to do business in localities. Because municipalities need jobs and resources, they will provide significant subsidies in order to attract capital or keep capital from moving away.

employers. Their presence stimulated entire local economies through their employment of local residents, procurement of local businesses, and a presence that provided stability in their regions. They were economic engines. In some cases, manufacturing firms still play a vital role in local economies. Retail firms were also among the most significant employers in prior generations.

But economies shifted. Many corporations in manufacturing and retail downsized, moved seeking lower operating costs, or simply became victims of a changed global economy fuelled by knowledge and technology. In the wake of these shifts, it became increasingly apparent that in numerous localities and regions, institutions of higher education and hospitals became the most significant local employers. Their significant landholdings, and overall endurance in local communities were also noticeable. Consequently, local populations, community organizations, and local governments began to ask more of these stable local assets – anchor institutions[4].

Defining Anchor Institutions

The AITF sees anchor institutions as enduring organizations that remain in their geographical settings and play a vital role in their local communities and economies. These are entities of varying types that have a stable presence, often over generations, in their neighbourhoods, cities, and regions. Consistent with AITF's values-orientation, the network sees anchor institutions as both objectively rooted geographically and subjectively committed to improving their surroundings. Indeed, institution can maintain a longstanding presence in a locality without actively collaborating and seeking to improve the community. An anchor institution both remains in place and recognizes the significance of its role as a local actor.

The definition of anchor institutions continues to evolve. Some definitions have suggested anchor institutions are only large organizations that are among the most significant local employers. Anchor institutions include the largest local employers. However, there

---

[4] AITF produces periodic literature reviews on decades of writing on anchor institutions, which discuss the continually increasing body of literature on the topic and the evolution of thinking on the idea of anchor institutions. To see AITF's last literature review: https://www.margainc.com/wp-content /uploads/2017/04/AITF_Literature_Review_2015_v_1.pdf, accessed January 27, 2019.

are some organizations that are not substantial in size, but they are enduring, and continually positioned to play a vital role in their communities and local economies.

The core of the anchor institutions movement has focused on urban areas. There are many reasons for this. Urban areas include, and will continue to include, the most substantial populations. The greatest global challenges are magnified in urban settings. The concentration of urban populations contributes to the scale of challenges as well as the opportunity to improve numerous lives.

However, the idea of enduring organizations remaining in their communities needing to expand their role in reviving localities is not exclusively urban. Many institutions of higher education, libraries, corporations, arts and cultural organizations, philanthropic institutions, and others are essential assets in rural communities. Many rural communities have been especially devastated by capital flight, which has only contributed to increased urbanization, as numerous rural residents have vacated their home communities, seeking opportunities in urban regions.

As the flight of capital from for profit corporations in manufacturing and other industries has been an important factor spawning the contemporary anchor institutions movement, there is some sentiment that for-profit corporations are not reliable local assets, and therefore, unable to be anchor institutions. Some suggest that since the preeminent anchor institutions of our times are institutions of higher education, hospitals, arts and cultural organizations, and other non-profit/non-governmental organizations, private corporations are not anchor institutions. It certainly may be the case that private corporations are inherently more mobile than entities such as universities. The profit motive may render some corporations unable to commit to place, as they will constantly seek to improve margins by seeking tax breaks, moving to other localities, eliminating jobs, and other pursuits common in business. AITF's definition, which emphasizes an organization's philosophy and values, suggests that a corporation can consciously commit to its locality. Some corporations are deeply engaged in their communities and consciously recognizing their role as a local actor.

The reality of anchor institutions is that their presence in place thrusts them into an interdependent relationship with their surroundings. Therefore, a corporation can benefit from its locality by hiring locally and reducing commuting times for employees or working to improve local schools that will pay future dividends in the skillsets of local residents. Institutions of higher education, hospitals, and anchors representing various fields are all interdependent with their localities. Consequently, if they are rooted in their neighbourhoods, cities, and regions, they best served by working to improve these surroundings. An anchor institution understands these dynamics.

It is also important to note that the concept of anchor institutions refers to organizations comprehensively – both in their core mission and in the corporate makeup. An institution of higher education, for example, is an engaged anchor institution when its pursuit of knowledge, through research and teaching, are is applied[5] to address critical issues in communities and its roles as an employer, purchaser, and real estate developer are harnessed to strengthen localities. Earlier iterations of the engagement of higher education focused on pieces of how universities are engaged (i.e. the civic engagement of students). The anchor movement merged the corporate and academic components of community partnerships, stressing the participation of the whole institution.

Anchor Institutions and the Local Mission of Higher Education

Higher education is a multifaceted field, including an array of different types of institutions, such as large private research universities, small private colleges, public universities, community colleges, and various other formations. These institutions have different priorities, but they all exist in localities. Some institutions of higher education are comprised of students from their immediate geographic areas, while some others are international. All institutions of higher education have a mission, which usually includes some commitment to producing knowledge for societal benefit. The local mission of higher education is an extension of this historical purpose of colleges and universities. This mission is demonstrated in a wide variety of ways among colleges and universities.

---

[5] Benson, Harkavy et al. (2017) argue for a transformation of institutions of higher education to deepen their commitment to public engagement and civic action. While we are witnesses the growth and development of an anchor institutions in which colleges and universities are central, many leaders in the field see the need for continuous attention to increasing the higher education's commitment to the kinds of values that AITF espouses.

The context that led to the emergence of the contemporary anchor institutions movement challenged colleges and universities to go further and transcend their existing programs and make a more comprehensive commitment to their communities. Many of the institutions that have been doing exemplary work in their communities are represented in AITF and continuing to make important contributions to their communities and the movement.

The University of Pennsylvania (Penn) – a large private research university in Philadelphia - has been a leader on numerous fronts. This institution has become known for its comprehensive approach to local engagement. The university provides hundreds of service learning classes and engages numerous faculty members in applying their expertise to addressing challenges in Philadelphia communities. It also has been investing in the local community by building the capacity of and contracting with local businesses and hiring locally. Penn has maintained a high level of commitment[6] to the local community at the level of the President for three consecutive administrations.

Augsburg University – a relatively small private university in Minneapolis – has leveraged its role as a local leader by helping to catalyze the engagement of other anchor institutions in the community. Augsburg works with other institutions of higher education, hospitals, and philanthropy in multi-institutional partnerships. The Central Corridor Anchor Partnership[7] brings these partners together to increase employment and educational opportunities locally.

Rutgers University Newark – a public urban university based in Newark within the Rutgers University State university system – has developed comprehensive goals to strengthen opportunities for

---

[6] Over the last twenty-five years, the Netter Center for Community Partnerships at Penn, founded by Ira Harkavy, has been organizing Academically Based Community Service courses to help faculty and students work together to solve challenging problems facing the local community. The Netter Center has also developed University Assisted Community Schools, which have been serving students and broader communities in the surrounding West Philadelphia area. Overall, the Center is committed to an anchor institution strategy to encourage mutually beneficial partnerships between universities, other anchor institutions, and their communities. For more on the Netter Center: https://www.nettercenter.upenn.edu/

[7] https://www.centralcorridoranchorpartnership.org/, accessed January 27, 2019.

Newark residents. The University has repurposed structures in Newark's downtown, developed an Honors Living Learning Community[8], and collaborated with numerous other local anchor institutions to increase local hiring and purchasing as well as attract more outsiders to move to Newark. The University helped create the Newark Anchor Collaborative, which enhances the capability of local anchor institutions to stimulate equitable growth in the city.

All of these institutions demonstrate how colleges and universities as anchor institutions can leverage their resources and expertise to improve local communities. This local engagement only enhances their mission institutions of higher education and their civic responsibilities as corporate entities. Additionally, place takes on a particular character in higher education. The ability of institutions of higher education to provide an enriching environment for students, faculty members, and staff is significantly shaped by place. Colleges and universities that are engaged anchors are acknowledging this reality.

The Future of the Anchor Institutions Movement
Looking to the future of how institutions of higher education participate in their communities as anchors, it is important to assess the quality and nature of this role. AITF continues to consider how to continually expand the anchor institutions movement as well as challenge anchor institutions to uphold AITF's values. Recently, AITF reflected on some areas to explore further upon the network's tenth anniversary. These are some areas recently identified as important to address as the anchor institutions movement enters a new phase of development.

Building a movement around a cross sector concept
The AITF's values orientation holds anchor institutions across sectors to a standard. It is important for anchor institutions to engage in their communities; but beyond their singular self-interest. Multi-anchor institution partnerships that connect numerous anchor institutions beyond their particular external initiatives are proliferating. In order to demonstrably improve the most pressing issues facing communities, no single anchor institution's programmes are sufficient. The ability to

---

[8] For more on the Honors Living Learning Community, see: https://hllc.newark.rutgers.edu/, accessed January 27, 2019.

transcend a single institution's interests and forge partnerships across institutions of higher education, hospitals, arts and cultural organizations, community-based organizations, government, business, philanthropy, and others is important to the future of neighbourhoods, municipalities, and regions. Therefore, AITF continues to encourage these multi-faceted partnerships. AITF brings representatives of different fields together around a common theme focusing on leveraging stable local assets to strengthen communities through democratic partnerships.

Sustaining a movement and a level of commitment among anchors

AITF stimulates mutual learning across its membership, facilitated largely by conferences, in order to improve practice on the ground. However, an anchor institution that is an engaged local actor will not necessarily remain committed to local communities and AITF's values. There are no guarantees. Dedication to these values has to be embedded in institutions and able to transcend leadership transitions. AITF has begun to think more proactively about building a pipeline of next generation leaders who would be positioned to sustain the work. Additionally, changes at the community level can threaten the sustainability of effective local partnerships as well. Governments and administrations change. Leadership changes take place among other anchor institutions as well as community-based organizations. Attention to how to sustain anchor partnerships is a continuous priority.

Equitable growth

Significant development projects have been stimulated by anchor institution community partnerships. In some instances, these efforts have revitalized communities. Sometimes revitalization leads to gentrification and displacement. AITF encourages community and economic development pursuits of anchor institutions to strongly consider equity throughout their practices. AITF's commitment to engagement is people-centred – prioritizing mutually beneficial collaboration that stresses the needs of community residents, particularly those who are most vulnerable. Inequities are manifested in numerous forms. Substantial economic inequality leads to tremendous differences in the distribution of resources and power. When anchor institutions' engagements in communities are people-centred, they are more likely to directly address various manifestations of inequality including race, ethnicity, gender, and other persistent areas by which power is distributed. Anchor institutions must avoid exacerbating inequality, and deliberately build and sustain inclusive and equitable community partnerships.

AITF and Policy

There is much more to consider looking to the future of the role of anchor institutions in their communities. Aligning the engagement of anchor institutions with local government can be an important way to increase the scale and impact of anchor institutions on issues such as health, education, economic opportunity and other areas. At a national level, it is important to consider how to incorporate the potential contributions of anchor institutions in community and economic development into policy. In higher education, for example, national policy expectations of higher education can include community partnerships. This context provides incentives for institutions of higher education to contribute to their communities. AITF recognizes the importance of promoting policy[9] at all levels of government in order to expand and incentivize anchor institutions' engagement in their communities. The AITF was created with a group of people writing a report to the U.S. Department of Housing and Urban Development in late 2009 (Harkavy et al. 2009). This particular agency, through programmes such as the Community Outreach Partnership Centers (COPC), helped lay the groundwork for the state of anchor field today by providing grants to help colleges and university apply research to

---

[9] AITF's policy approach began with an emphasis on the U.S. Department of Housing and Urban Development. Gradually, efforts to influence U.S. policy at the Federal level, focused on the U.S. Department of Education, and the White House (prior to 2017). Over time, AITF recognized that anchor institutions are relevant across issues and government agencies. The issues of concern to education, health, commerce, the environment, and beyond are manifested in localities. Considering the range of types of anchor institutions, there are numerous roles anchor institutions can play in relation to multiple issues at various levels of government. AITF hopes government agencies of all types will consider anchor institutions are valuable resources and potential partners. Because of this evolution in thinking, AITF's policy strategy is multifaceted. At this current stage, AITF is more heavily emphasizing deeper collaboration between anchor institutions and municipal governments.

improving their localities. The local level of government has become increasingly important to AITF. It has been collaborating with organizations such as the National League of Cities and highlighting ways in which anchor institutions and local governments can collaborate.

AITF and Philanthropy

While government incentives have played an important role in advancing anchor institution community partnerships, private philanthropy has been crucial in providing capital to help launch and sustain multi-institutional partnerships. Community foundations have been acting as engaged anchor institutions with a unique ability to convene across sectors and industries. In some cases, private philanthropists have provided support to anchor institutions as stable partners that can help pursue issues they care about (i.e. strengthening local schools). Since its inception, AITF has been stressing alignment between the anchor institutions movement and philanthropy. Philanthropists/philanthropic institutions and anchor institutions can pursue the same goals simultaneously. Anchor institutions could provide ways to sustain and stabilize the initiatives in which philanthropy invests.

Becoming even more global

Another important goal of the anchor institutions movement is to become increasingly global. The contemporary concept of anchor institutions has been increasingly referenced and applied in numerous fields in the United States. Most notably, in the last decade alone, the anchor institutions movement has spread well beyond higher education. The dynamics of organizations that endure in their localities is universal. It is a global idea to leverage stable local assets for community and economic development.

The meeting in Dublin between AITF, the Council of Europe and Dublin City University in October 2018 was an important event towards the further globalization of the anchor institutions movement. A series of conversations among European higher education leaders has emerged. Higher education is a logical place to catalyze exchanges on anchor institutions as local actors in Europe. Opportunities to organize similar discussions on institutions of higher education as local actors have been evolving in South Africa and Australia. These kinds of discussions have been widening the network of those discussing these issues.

Conclusion

Overall, the anchor institutions movement is at a turning point. The AITF, as the movement organization, will continue to move this work to new stages of development. Continuing to encourage anchor institution community partnerships is important, and perhaps essential to the future of communities. Limited resources in government, persistent inequities manifested in localities, fluid or unstable local economies are dynamics that highlight the need for institutions that are rooted in their communities to increase their commitment to their communities. The future of local communities depends on the continued local engagement of anchor institutions.

REFERENCES

Benson, L., Harkavy, I., Puckett, J., Hartley, M., Hodges, R., Johnston, F. & Weeks, J. (2017): *Knowledge for Social Change: Bacon, Dewey, and the Revolutionary Transformation of Research Universities in the Twenty-First Century*. Philadelphia, PA: Temple University Press.

CEOs for Cities (2010): How To Behave Like an Anchor Institution. Available at https://ceosforcities.org/wp-content/uploads/2015/12/How-To-Behave-Like-An-Anchor-Institution.pdf, accessed January 27, 2019.

Dragicevic, N. (2015): Prosperous Province: Strategies For Building Community Wealth. https://tspace.library.utoronto.ca/bitstream/1807/80124/5/Dragicevic_2015_Anc hor Institutions.pdf, accessed January 29, 2019

Dubb, S., and Howard, T. (2012): Leveraging Anchor Institutions for Local Job Creation and Wealth Building. Available at https://community-wealth.org/sites/clone.community-wealth.org/files/downloads/paper-dubb-howard_0.pdf, accessed January 27, 2019.

Harkavy I. et al., Anchor Institutions as Partners in Building Successful Communities and Local Economies", in Retooling HUD for a Catalytic Federal Government: A Report to Secretary Shaun Donovan. Available at https://www.margainc.com/wp-content/uploads/2017/05/Retooling-HUD-Chap ter-8.pdf, accessed January 28, 2019

Maurrasse, D. (2007) "City Anchors: Leveraging Anchor Institutions for Urban Success. White Paper. CEOs for Cities" September 2007 Available at: https://community-wealth.org/content/city-anchors-leveraging-anchor-institutions-urban-success, accessed January 29, 2019

Rivlin, A., and O'Cleireacain, C. (2001): "In the District of Columbia: Families vs. singles, costs vs. benefits". The Washington Post, July 1, 2001, B03.

INSTITUTIONAL PERSPECTIVES

CHAPTER 3
THE UNIVERSITY AND LOCAL CIVIC ENGAGEMENT: AN IRISH CASE STUDY

Joanna Ozarowska

Introduction

The global history of university–community engagement in pursuit of enhanced citizenship highlights its importance in terms of defining university identity and in promoting sustainable cities and regions. For this citizenship strategy to be effective and durable, it requires deliberate and mutually determined collaboration between all sections of the university community (academic staff, administrative staff and students) and the wider community. Over and beyond this 'buy in' from all sections of the university and the community, there is the need for this strategy to be put into practice, as well as stated in principle. It is all very well for citizenship/community strategies to feature in strategic and mission statements, but these need to be embedded and mainstreamed in academic and student culture for them to deliver on their promise. This chapter examines an Irish case study, that of Dublin City University, located in an area of marked social disadvantage but also noted for its proactive and impactful engagement with its local community.

The Irish Landscape

Over the past decade in Ireland, the role higher education institutions play in local communities has been given more attention, particularly with the establishment of Campus Engage[1] – a formal network of HEIs, modelled on the US Campus Compact, tasked with promoting the social and civic mission of higher education - in 2007.

While the founding of the network led to more concerted efforts for the higher education system to engage with local public, statutory and community partners to address pressing societal issues, even before then a number of early initiatives, led from the ground up by engaged scholars and practitioners, were in existence. These 'pockets of excellence' have included Community Knowledge Initiative (CKI)[2] -

---

[1] www.campusengage.ie, accessed February 15, 2019
[2] https://cki.nuigalway.ie/, accessed February 15, 2019

established in 2001 at National University of Ireland Galway (NUIG); the Shannon Consortium[3] - formed by four higher education institutions in the Limerick and Kerry region; Students Learning with Communities[4] office, which in 2008 consolidated local engagement initiatives at Dublin Institute of Technology; and DCU in the Community[5] - a community outreach centre linked with Dublin City University - first opened in 2008 after a number of years of consultations with community and statutory partners.

A significant development in national policy came in 2011 with the publication of the National Strategy for Higher Education to 2030 which explicitly recognized engagement with society as a core part of higher education sector mission:

> "Engagement with the wider community must become more firmly embedded in the mission of higher education institutions. Higher education institutions need to become more firmly embedded in the social and economic contexts of the communities they live in and serve" (Department of Education and Skills, 2011: 77).

This policy development legitimized and endorsed the existing and emerging initiatives addressing the social mission of higher education. Not only did it serve as leverage for securing further funding both from the government and individual higher education institutions to develop local community engagement activities, but it also ultimately led to their inclusion within the Higher Education Performance Framework with specific key performance indicators for individual institutions. The launch of the Campus Engage 'Charter for Higher Education Civic and Community Engagement'[6], signed in 2014 by the Presidents of the 20 Irish universities and institutes of technology, further provided a foundation for developing more concerted efforts to build and embed this area across Irish higher education sector.

---

[3] https://www3.ul.ie/cemtl/shannonConsortium.htm, accessed February 15, 2019

[4] http://www.dit.ie/ace/studentslearningwithcommunities/, accessed February 15, 2019

[5] https://www.dcu.ie/community/about.shtml, accessed February 15, 2019

[6] http://www.campusengage.ie/userfiles/files/Campus%20Engage%20Charter _June%20Final.pdf, accessed February 15, 2019

Dublin City University

Dublin City University was one of the first higher education institutions in Ireland to develop and launch an explicit civic and community engagement policy as part of the University's 2005-2008 Leadership Through Foresight strategy. Pursuing active engagement with surrounding communities has been a significant feature of every DCU strategic plan since. While some higher education institutions might put less emphasis on the geographical location they inhabit, Dublin City University has recognized the importance of its immediate surrounding area and has made concerted efforts to engage with local stakeholders through creating mutually beneficial partnerships and links (Munck et al 2012; O'Broin 2010). It has been argued (ibid.), that DCU is geographically 'well-placed' to realize its social mission – the areas immediately to the north of the university have experienced an extremely high level of social and economic disadvantage and exclusion. The 2016 Deprivation Index report by Pobal[7], considering factors such as unemployment, social class composition, educational attainment levels and housing, designates a number of areas on the Dublin Northside bordering the university (especially Ballymun, Finglas, Kilmore, Darndale and Coolock) as considerably disadvantaged (Haase & Pratschke 2017, Pobal 2016) without much amelioration visible.

Community and civic engagement at Dublin City University includes a spectrum of practices that permeate the university's operations, teaching and learning activities, and research. These practices are embedded in DCU's culture and workings to varying extents and include public and media engagement; sustainability; widening access and participation; community-based learning; engaged research; student and staff volunteerism; involvement in community development, economic and social regeneration; and education for active citizenship. Staff and students' contribution in these areas is recognized and showcased annually through DCU President's Awards for Engagement, now in its 10th year up and running. Many of these activities are focused on engagement with regional, national, and even international communities, as well as those in the closely surrounding areas. Perhaps the most tangible manifestation of Dublin City University's engagement with its very

---

[7] https://www.pobal.ie, accessed February 15, 2019

immediate community is the DCU in the Community outreach centre, situated within a short physical distance from the University's main campus, but separated from it socially, economically and culturally.

DCU in the Community

Established in 2008 (and re-opened in 2010), DCU in the Community is located in Ballymun – an area on the Northside of Dublin. In 1960s, the area saw the development of the Ballymun Estate – a housing scheme comprising large residential flat complexes, including high-rise tower blocks, built to alleviate the severe housing crisis in Dublin inner city at that time (Somerville-Woodward 2002). Initially hailed as a success, over the following decades the scheme became a significant urban planning failure – the lack of amenities for the residents, poor transport links, scarcity of schools, and overcrowding in housing units, coupled with few employment prospects led to the emergence of significant social issues, including crime and substance abuse (ibid.). That in turn translated into the area experiencing extremely high levels of social deprivation and exclusion in terms of unemployment, housing and educational prospects. The state had set up Ballymun Regeneration Limited (BRL) in 1997 to drive a physical regeneration (housing and amenities) programme, which is now largely completed; however, it is recognized that the social regeneration aspect was neglected. As the only higher education institution in the area, Dublin City University, under its civic engagement strategy launched in 2006, forged a partnership with BRL and committed to use its resources to help drive social regeneration through education, which would enhance capacity locally and drive social capital formation, through the opening of DCU in the Community centre. Local community involvement was considered to be crucial from the very beginning in terms of providing a structured input to develop the vision, mission and goals for the newly established centre.

DCU in the Community's original mission was to provide educational and lifelong learning opportunities to local residents in order to promote equality in third level education and to broaden access to higher education among underrepresented groups – "second chance" learners, mature students, and learners from socio-economically disadvantaged areas. In the following years, the spectrum of civic engagement activities offered at DCU in the Community has broadened significantly, and currently also includes student volunteering, community-based learning and community-engaged research, as well as a range of ad hoc local community-university projects.

Outcomes and Impact

With only three full-time staff members, the DCU in the Community model is low-cost/high impact. Nearly a decade since the centre's re-launch in 2010, it displays a strong positive balance sheet in all of its activities[8] . DCU in the Community is firmly established on the local community map and well-networked among community and voluntary sector organizations; the centre also enjoys steadily increasing 'buy-in' among DCU staff and students.

Between 2010 and the present, DCU in the Community has delivered over 80 accredited and non-accredited learning programmes for local residents in the areas of college preparation, digital media, social studies, psychology, health and wellbeing, personal finance, mathematics, and sports and fitness, with a majority of the programmes delivered in partnership with local community and voluntary organizations. Over 1,200 community learners and adults returning to education have enrolled in the programmes. Additionally, staff at the centre have provided 150-180 hours annually of educational guidance and mentoring for adults returning to education – both in-house students and external clients. DCU in the Community has assisted with more than 200 applications to full time further and higher education for mature students and adult learners from socio-economically disadvantaged areas, contributing to the increase in the levels of participation in the local community. However, the impact of DCU in the Community activities in the local community goes beyond progression in education and opportunity to obtain accredited further education awards in a community setting. The impact on individuals who have availed themselves of the programmes and supports at the centre represents the most personal and human aspect of DCU's local civic engagement. The majority of those individuals would have left formal education early and experienced some level of marginalization in mainstream education. Many have been unable to access further learning options due to personal, social, cultural or financial

---

[8] DCU in the Community Annual Reports available at: https://www.dcu.ie/community/publications.shtml, accessed February 15, 2019

circumstances. For a large proportion of our students, walking through DCU in the Community door was the first time in years when they had an opportunity to engage in learning. Greater interest in education (own and children's) and increased awareness of the value of third level and lifelong learning, in a community where traditionally few could access and benefit from the cultural and social resources of the university, cannot be overstated. Empowerment, improved well-being, social mobility and employability are also all additional outcomes for a local community that has coped with adversity and engaged decisively with higher education as a pathway out of social exclusion and marginalization. The voices of DCU in the Community students perhaps reflect this best:

Attending DCU in the Community was the best personal decision I could have ever made. Initially I went to meet people and make friends. But it turned out to be so much more. It gave me the confidence to continue my education and realize I wasn't as stupid as I thought I was. It is such a great launching pad into further education. I am now studying at DCU. The opportunities that are open to me there are endless. I am thoroughly enjoying it even though it is such a huge challenge. This was all due to the fact that I went to DCU in the Community. I would recommend that anyone try this free facility and see what you are capable of and how willing and helpful the staff are (Janet)

DCU in the Community is the most helpful facility. The staff are very professional and always there to offer guidance. The advice I got from DCU in the Community helped me with my future choices and now I have been accepted for third level education in DCU. I can't imagine myself being where I am now without assistance of DCU in the Community (Maria)

Returning to education as a mature student seemed a little daunting to me at first, but that soon passed as I began to really enjoy working with like-minded students. DCU in the Community gave me the confidence and practical help to successfully begin studying for a degree at Dublin City University (Tony)

I found the course great for my preparation to go on to third level education. It really got me focused on learning and helped so much with my confidence. I have learned a lot on the course and enjoyed my time here, and have met some wonderful people (David)

I feel I am ready to go on to further education and have the confidence and belief that I can succeed. I didn't have this belief before doing this course. It feels I know more now of what is expected of me in third level education (Stephen)

I had been taking baby steps since returning to education as an adult, after finishing the course I felt that I now had the confidence and self-belief to take the last big step, and apply for a degree (Valerie)[9]

It would of course be unjust and impossible to credit DCU in the Community itself for these achievements - all activities in the centre have been delivered in partnership with a network of local organizations - from community education providers and schools, through local partnership companies and employment centres, drug and alcohol services, to parents' groups and residents associations. Last but not least, the support of and input from DCU senior staff, academics and students also contributed greatly to the centre's successes.

Separately, DCU in the Community, on behalf of DCU, has co-led (jointly with University of Limerick, the National University of Ireland Galway and Campus Engage) the development of *Student Volunteer[10]* – a national higher education student volunteering management system. Between 2010 and present close to 1,000 DCU students from across all DCU Schools and Faculties have been linked with volunteering and service learning opportunities in the local community - many of the students led the development of new volunteering opportunities in consultation with community partners and based on community needs. Student engagement, leadership, and volunteering activities promoted by DCU in the Community have provided DCU students with an

---

[9] Selection of testimonies collected by the author as part of internal DCU in the Community student course evaluation forms 2011-2018
[10] www.studentvolunteer.ie, accessed February 15, 2019

opportunity to develop graduate attributes, such as creativity and enterprise, problem solving, communication skills, community and global awareness, and leadership.

In terms of the 'value' of this engagement, a pilot study was conducted at DCU in 2014 to estimate the economic and social value of the university's civic engagement activities[11] . The methodology used - socially modified economic value (SMEV) - was adapted to capture the economic weight of DCU's local engagement activities, with those delivered in disadvantaged areas "worth" more in terms of the social value generated (Munck et al 2015). According to the report, the total value generated by DCU in the Community itself in 2012 stood at over €400k which exceeds the budget for the centre (inputs) over two-fold. It is worth considering that these figures represent the value generated by DCU in the Community only through the delivery of educational programmes and student volunteering; the social value produced by the whole range of the centre's activities would certainly be even higher. This shows, for us, that civic engagement is not a drain on university resources as some might think.

Challenges and prospects
Despite the successes of the centre and the increasing embeddedness of civic engagement within Dublin City University's strategic plans, it has been a challenge to maintain DCU in the Community itself as a strategic priority. While the level of 'buy in' from staff and students has steadily increased and in terms of funding, the partnership between DCU and Dublin City Council makes sense to both parties in terms of addressing the ongoing problems of the deprived areas of the city, the resource allocation issue remains. The voice and support of the local community have been crucial in maintaining the university's support for DCU in the Community, especially throughout the recent economic crisis. This is congruent with the experience in other countries (see Géstsdóttir, Kistryn, Weeks, and Wildova et al. in this volume) that stresses the importance of the two-way process of knowledge dissemination and exchange between the university and the local community.

---

[11] Available at: https://www.dcu.ie/sites/default/files/community/pdfs/Report 2014.pdf, accessed February 15, 2019

For many local communities, the university is perceived as an island or 'enclave' somewhat divorced from local needs. But as universities across Europe have developed new ways of breaking down barriers between the academic 'enclave' and the local community, they have sought new ways to present themselves. In this way they seek to reinforce the role of the university as a key urban institution: not an enclave of learning that happens to find itself in a city but rather a key element of the city. They become 'anchor institutions' (Maurrasse in this volume) in a very real sense. This development is a crucial part of the process whereby universities help localities engage with the sometimes challenging globalizing processes facing them. These new and demanding political and socio-economic environments tend to produce competitive pressures in terms of universities international rankings that do not necessarily reflect the true value of an anchor institution embedded in its local community.

The engaged university recognizes that it is part of the community around it. The success of a university is very often completely intertwined with the prospects of the community of which it is a part. A thriving university boosts the town or city in which it is situated. Likewise, a dynamic city is good news for any university trying to make its mark in a global knowledge system. The productive interaction and mutual engagement between the university and the wider community are beneficial to both in many ways. It is now increasingly acknowledged that universities can play an important role in terms of community development, in support of civil society, in a knowledge-based global economy, and in a socially challenged world (Watson et al 2011, Munck et al 2012, Bergan and Harkavy 2018). This can lead to enhanced human and social capital development, improved professional infrastructure and capacity-building and, more broadly, to benefits for the socio-economic, environmental and cultural dimensions of the wider community.

References

Bergan, S. and Harkavy, I. (eds.) (2018). *Higher Education for Diversity, Social Inclusion and Community. A Democratic Imperative*. Council of Europe Higher Education Series No. 22. Strasbourg: Council of Europe Publishing.

Department of Education and Skills. (2011). National Strategy for Higher Education to 2030. Dublin: DES.

Géstsdóttir, S. (this volume): "The University of Iceland's Participation in the Local and National Community: Increasing Impact, Widening Access"

Haase, T. and Pratschke, J. (2017). The 2016 Pobal HP Deprivation Index for Small Areas (SA) Introduction and Reference Tables. Retrieved February 6, 2019 from https://www.pobal.ie/app/uploads/2018/06/The-2016-Pobal-HP-Deprivation-Index-Introduction-07.pdf

Kistryn, S. (this volume):" A Traditional University in its Local Community: the Jagiellonian University in Kraków"

Maurrasse, D. (this volume): "What Is an Anchor Institution and Why?"

Munck, R., Kelly, U., and Ozarowska, J. (2015). The Value of Civic Engagement in Higher Education: An Irish Case Study. Retrieved February 8, 2019 from https://www.dcu.ie/sites/default/files/community/pdfs/Value.pdf

Munck, R., McQuillan, H. and Ozarowska, J. Civic Engagement in Cold Climate: A Glocal Perspective in McIlrath, L., Lyons, A., Munck, R. (eds.). (2012). *Higher Education and Civic Engagement: Comparative Perspectives*. New York: Palgrave MacMillan, pp. 15-29.

O'Broin, D. Civic Engagement: Core Business or Add On? in Munck, R. and Mohrman, K. (eds.). (2010). *Reinventing The University: Creating A New Vision*. Dublin: DCU Press at Glasnevin Publishing, pp. 91-100.

Somerville-Woodward, R. (2002). Ballymun: A History. Dublin: BRL. Retrieved February 6, 2019 from http://www.brl.ie/pdf/ballymun_a_history_1600_ 1997_synopsis.pdf

Watson, D., Hollister, R., Stroud, S. and Babcock, E. (eds.) (2011) *The Engaged University: International Perspectives on Civic Engagement*. New York and London: Routledge

Weeks, J. (this volume): "Campus and Community Revitalization in the United States: Penn's Evolution as an Anchor Institution"

Wildová, R., Fliegel T. and Vokšická B. (this volume): "The Third Mission of Universities: Examples of Good Practice from the Czech Republic"

CHAPTER 4
CAMPUS AND COMMUNITY REVITALISATION IN THE UNITED STATES: PENN'S EVOLUTION AS AN ANCHOR INSTITUTION[1]

Joann Weeks

"The picture that emerges is one of a relationship in which the University and the City are important to one another. We stand on common ground, our futures very much intertwined."

- University of Pennsylvania Annual Report, 1987-88: Penn and Philadelphia: Common Ground

"At Penn, local engagement is one of the core tenets of the Penn Compact — Penn's Strategic Vision for moving from excellence to eminence — and is an integral part of the University's mission."

University of Pennsylvania Financial Report, 2008-2009

Introduction

Recognizing and realizing its position as an anchor institution in West Philadelphia, Penn's local geographic community, and in Philadelphia more generally, did not come readily to the University of Pennsylvania. It was a 20-plus year trajectory from President Sheldon Hackney's initial acknowledgement in the 1987-88 Annual Report that the fate of Penn and the City were inextricably linked, to President Amy Gutmann's full embrace of local engagement as "an integral part of the University's mission." As described in this article, civic engagement

---

[1] This article draws significantly from *Knowledge for Social Change: Bacon, Dewey and the Revolutionary Transformation of Research Universities in the Twenty-First Century* (2017) by Lee Benson, Ira Harkavy, John Puckett, Matthew Hartley, Rita A. Hodges, Francis E. Johnston and Joann Weeks, Philadelphia, PA: Temple University Press. It also draws from "Engaging Urban Universities as Anchor Institutions for Health Equity," by Ira Harkavy, in American Journal for Public Health, Vol. 106 (12), December 2016 and "University-Community Partnerships in Pursuit of Social Justice: An Anchor Institutions Approach to Advancing Teaching and Research and Improving the Quality of Life" by Ira Harkavy and Rita A. Hodges for Rutgers University-Camden Symposium, January 2018.

has increasingly moved from the periphery to the core of Penn's work. It has required presidential and faculty leadership; integration of local engagement in the university's academic mission, and its role as a corporate citizen; development of mutually beneficial, mutually respectful partnerships with the community; and creation of organizational units and operational integration within the University to sustain the commitment over time.

The Penn/Philadelphia context

The extreme poverty, persistent deprivation, and pernicious racism afflicting communities in the shadows of powerful, relatively wealthy urban universities raise troubling moral issues, as well as questions about higher education's contribution to the public good. It is essential that universities as key anchor institutions significantly and effectively contribute to radically reducing the pervasive, on-going, seemingly intractable problems of our inner cities (Harkavy et al. 2009).

Conditions in Penn's city, Philadelphia, Pennsylvania are an example of a more general phenomenon of urban distress. At approximately 25.7 percent, the poverty rate is the highest among the nation's 10 largest cities. About 400,000 residents—including roughly 37 percent of the city's children under the age of 18—live below the federal poverty line, which is $19,337 in annual income for an adult living with two children. And nearly half of all poor residents are in deep poverty, defined as 50 percent below the federal poverty line (The Pew Charitable Trusts 2017). At the same time, Philadelphia (and many other cities) is home to a key resource that can help to change these conditions. It has one of the highest concentrations of anchor institutions, with "eds and meds"[2] representing 12 of the 15 largest private employers, and the Philadelphia metropolitan area contains more than 100 colleges and universities (Select Greater Philadelphia Council 2016).

Why universities as anchor institutions?

Leadership at Penn, and across higher education in the United States, has increasingly recognized that there is a significant rationale for

---

[2] "Eds and Meds" denotes college and universities as well as academic medical centers and hospitals.

universities to be partners in community revitalization. Higher education institutions cannot hold themselves aloof from their communities. The fate of the university and its host communities and cities are intertwined. Given their resources, particularly their human capital — faculty, staff and students — universities can make significant contributions to the quality of life in their local communities and cities. And finally, through local engagement universities can enhance their overall mission of teaching, research, and service by striving to improve the quality of life in their host communities and cities.

Universities are rooted institutions. Given their physical assets it is less likely that they will move. They are also among the largest purchasers of goods and services and, as noted above, among the largest employers in their region. Penn is the largest private employer in the City of Philadelphia. With the range of employment at a university, they attract highly skilled individuals and related businesses.

A burgeoning democratic civic and community engagement movement within higher education has developed in part as a response to these pervasive problems. Service learning, community-based participatory research, volunteer projects, and community economic development initiatives are some of the means that have been used to create mutually beneficial partnerships designed to make a positive difference in the community and on campus. But these efforts, although they are important, generally fall far short of what is required.

An urban university's interaction with its local community might usefully be placed within the following four categories:

1. Gentrification and displacement of low-income residents,
2. Disregard and neglect,
3. Partially engaged (frequently indicated by involvement of the academic or the institutional/corporate component of the university, but not both),
4. Truly engaged (involving comprehensive, significant, serious, and sustained involvement of *all* aspects of the university with the community, including integration of academic and institutional resources).

We argue for the development of truly engaged universities, in which a very high priority is given not only to significantly improving the quality of life in the local community, but also to working with the community respectfully, collaboratively, and democratically. In addition, helping to develop and implement solutions to strategic, community-identified local problems functions as a curriculum, text, *and* performance test for a truly engaged university's research, teaching, and learning activities (Harkavy, Hartley et al. 2016). No urban university, as far as we can tell, presently meets these criteria. Nonetheless, progress has occurred over the past 30 or so years with an increasing number of universities taking meaningful, if insufficient, steps in the right direction. We turn to the efforts of the University of Pennsylvania, which has been recognized as a leader for its involvement with West Philadelphia, its local geographic community (Davis, 2015).

Towards an integrated democratic anchor institution-community partnerships approach

In her inaugural address in October 2004, Penn President Amy Gutmann announced a comprehensive "Penn Compact" (Compact) designed to advance the University from "excellence to eminence" (Gutmann 2004). Although the Compact's first two principles — increasing access to a Penn education and integrating knowledge — had, and continue to have, significant importance for Penn, the third principle of engaging locally and globally is particularly relevant to our purpose.

Gutmann's articulation of Penn's core values and aspirations in the Compact brought an increased emphasis to realizing the university's institutional potential through working to solve real-world problems in partnership with communities, while continuing to invest its economic resources locally. Local engagement work moved from being primarily a means to help Penn revitalise its local environment to becoming a way for it to achieve eminence as a research university. Moreover, the Compact's clear directive has become infused in nearly every aspect of the University, shaping both operations and culture across the campus.

The Netter Center for Community Partnerships

President Gutmann has also championed the work of the Netter Center for Community Partnerships[3], which was officially founded in 1992 by President Sheldon Hackney as the Center for Community Partnerships, but whose work in West Philadelphia began in the mid-1980s. Renamed through a major gift in 2007, the Netter Center works to identify, mobilize, and integrate Penn's vast resources in order to help transform West Philadelphia, particularly by improving the public schools while helping to transform teaching, research and service at the University.

The Center's work was building on efforts begun in the early 1980s, particularly the development of two core concepts: academically based community service and university-assisted community schools. Through Academically Based Community Service (ABCS) courses, service is rooted in and intrinsically tied to research, teaching, and learning, and the goal of these courses is to contribute to structural community improvement. University-Assisted Community Schools educate, engage, empower, and serve not only students, but also all other members of the community, providing an organising framework for bringing university programs, including ABCS courses, to West Philadelphia schools. The Netter Center has come to view ABCS and university-assisted community schools (UACS) as core to a comprehensive anchor institution strategy in which universities engage in sustained, mutually beneficial partnerships with their communities.

Since the early 1990s, an increasing number of faculty members, from a wide range of Penn schools and departments, have revised existing courses, or have created new ABCS courses, providing innovative curricular opportunities for their students to become active learners, creative real-world problem solvers, and active producers (as opposed to passive consumers) of knowledge. In 2017-2018, the Netter Center helped coordinate 68 ABCS courses taught in seven of Penn's 12 schools, engaging approximately 1700 Penn students (undergraduate, graduate, and professional).

On-going, faculty-led projects are important to sustaining the Netter Center's community engagement. The Agatston Urban Nutrition

---

[3] See https://www.nettercenter.upenn.edu/, accessed January 28, 2019.

Initiative[4] is an example of an evolving Netter Center programme that was catalysed through ABCS. In 1991, Professor Francis Johnston, a renowned expert on nutritional anthropology who had recently concluded a lengthy tenure as chair of the Anthropology Department decided to redesign a course, Anthropology 210, to address the community-identified problem of poor nutrition, with the initial work at Turner Middle School. It became the prototype for Academically Based Community Service courses. A widening circle of Penn faculty and students began working with Johnston over the next few years in collaboration with local middle school teachers and students to understand the nutritional practices in the community. The course also sought to address the problem through a series of projects aimed at encouraging better nutrition. These included an educational programme, a school-based garden, an in-school market that provided healthy snacks, and a nutritional outreach programme for the community. Anthropology 210's success not only influenced the anthropology department (which went on to develop an academic track on Public Interest Anthropology), but it also inspired other Penn departments and schools to become involved. Furthermore, it led to the development of the Agatston Urban Nutrition Initiative (AUNI). Today, AUNI integrates research, teaching, learning, and service in an approach that brings together a range of Penn's social science, health, and medical resources, as well as the resources of community partners at the Netter Center's UACS sites in West Philadelphia, at more than a dozen other Philadelphia schools, and at various West Philadelphia community centres and locations, to improve health and nutrition and reduce obesity (Johnston and Harkavy 2009; Benson, Harkavy et al. 2007).

As noted above, another major component of the Netter Center's work is mobilizing the substantial resources of the University to help traditional public schools serve as innovative university-assisted community schools that educate, engage, empower, and serve not only students, but also all members of the community in which the school is located. ABCS courses, internships, and work-study and volunteer opportunities bring hundreds of Penn students into the schools, where

---

[4] See http://www.nettercenter.upenn.edu/what-we-do/programs/university-assisted-community-schools/agatston-urban-nutrition-initiative, accessed January 28, 2019.

programming occurs during the school day, after school, evenings, and summers.

As of autumn 2018, the Netter Center's work has grown to include children and families at nine university-assisted community schools in West Philadelphia. Netter Center site directors collaborate closely with each school and its community to determine activities that best serve their specific needs and interests. In addition to coordinating the programmes, UACS site directors serve as liaisons between the university and the school, as well as between school day teachers and the afterschool programme. Staff from the Center's thematic-based programmes such as the Agatston Urban Nutrition Initiative.

However, academic engagement alone is insufficient to make the needed changes. The involvement of the entire university is called for if genuine progress is to be made. By beginning to consciously integrate its academic and its institutional efforts for community improvement, Penn is mobilising increased resources to better realize its mission as an engaged anchor institution. Some of Penn's community economic development efforts are described below.

Role of the Office of Executive Vice President in Community Economic Development

The Netter Center works in close partnership with the Office of Executive Vice President (EVP) on issues of community economic development that help advance Penn's role as an anchor institution. The EVP's office supports the academic and programmatic goals of the University by providing operational, financial, entrepreneurial, and environmental services to enhance the well-being and successes of faculty, students, staff and local community. A Planning Committee of Penn and community partners provides strategic oversight and direction regarding Penn's economic inclusion objectives.

Penn's Economic Inclusion Program engages local, minority, and women-owned businesses and residents in the university's economic activity. Penn launched its "Buy West Philadelphia" programme in the 1980s, for example, to direct its purchasing dollars to local vendors, and the programme has continued to grow since then. In fiscal year 2015, Penn spent $122 million with West Philadelphia–based businesses (approximately 13.07% of total purchasing of goods and services). (Office of the Executive Vice President 2015). Penn partners with city entities such as the Minority Business Enterprise Center to help build capacity for small, local suppliers. For all campus construction projects of five million dollars or more, Penn has also made it a condition of general contractors to hire at least 20% women or minority-owned subcontractors. In fiscal year 2015, Penn and its Health System hired 1572 local residents (47.5% of all new hires). In housing development, since 1998, Penn's Enhanced Mortgage Program has provided over 1,000 grants to staff and faculty as an incentive to choose West Philadelphia to live in. Penn also created a Neighborhood Preservation and Development Fund in the mid-90s to secure several hundred units of apartments to below market price, to ensure equity among housing, while also creating new market rate housing (Office of the Executive Vice President 2019).

Penn helped create a special services district – University City District (UCD) – in 1997 to clean the streets and help patrol alongside Penn's own police force and city police. Today, UCD is a 26-member board representing "eds and meds," local businesses and non-profits, and residents, chaired by Penn's executive vice president Craig Carnaroli, with a much broader vision. Between 2000 and 2016, UCD trained approximately 600 local residents for jobs at Penn and other local anchor institutions through its West Philadelphia Skills Initiative, with over 90% of recent graduates connected to employment (University City District 2016).

These strategies – including ABCS, UACS, and community economic development activities that help advance Penn's role as anchor institution – are shared with others across the country and around the world, including through the Anchor Institutions Task Force.

Obstacles to developing and sustaining democratic university-community partnerships

Although the work described at Penn indicates progress, Penn and other institutions of higher education still have a very long way to go to comprehensively and effectively engage and align their various components and substantial resources in democratic, sustained, mutually transformative partnerships with their local communities. Significant obstacles have impeded the development of truly engaged universities.

These impediments - including commercialism and commodification, misplaced nostalgia for traditional, elitist, "ivory tower" liberal arts education, and intellectual and institutional fragmentation - have slowed down Penn and other institutions' development as truly democratic, engaged, civic universities.

"Communities have problems, universities have departments," stated a report the Center for Educational Research and Innovation that was published by the Organisation for Economic Cooperation and Development (OECD) titled The University and the Community: The Problems of Changing Relationships (Center for Educational Research 1982:127). Beyond being a criticism of universities, that statement neatly indicates another major reason why colleges and universities have not contributed as they should. Quite simply, their unintegrated, fragmented, internally conflictual structure and organization impede understanding and developing solutions to highly complex human and societal problems. Colleges and universities need to significantly decrease the fragmentation of disciplines, overspecialization, and division between and among the arts and sciences and the professions, since these departmental and disciplinary divisions have increased the isolation of higher education from society itself. Compounding this problem is what might be called the "disciplinary fallacy" afflicting American universities, namely, the misconception that faculty members are duty-bound to serve only the scholastic interests and preoccupations of their disciplines and have neither the responsibility nor the capacity to help their universities keep their longstanding promise to prepare undergraduates for lives of moral and civic responsibility.[5]

These impediments have reinforced, in Benjamin Franklin's wonderful phrase, an "unaccountable prejudice in favor of ancient Customs and Habitudes", rather than helping to realize Franklin's original vision when founding the University of Pennsylvania to educate students with "an *Inclination* join'd with an *Ability* to serve Mankind, one's Country, Friends and Family [Original Emphasis]." (Franklin 1962).

---

[5] Stanley Fish is arguably the most outspoken proponent of the "disciplinary fallacy;" see his *Save the world on your time*. (2008) New York: Oxford University Press.

Reducing the obstacles

So, what is to be done to reduce the negative effects of dysfunctional traditions, commercialism and commodification, ivory tower nostalgia, and intellectual and institutional fragmentation?

Simply put, engage locally. As colleges and universities work collaboratively with members of their local communities on universal problems (such as poverty, health inequities, substandard housing, and inadequate, unequal education) that are manifested locally, they will be better able to advance learning, research, teaching, and service.

The benefits of a local community focus for college and university civic engagement programmes are manifold. Ongoing, continuous interaction is facilitated through work in an easily accessible location. Relationships of trust, so essential for effective partnerships and effective learning, are also built through day-to-day work on problems and issues of mutual concern. In addition, the local community provides a convenient setting in which service-learning courses, community-based research courses, and related courses in different disciplines can work together on a complex problem to produce substantive results. Work in a university's local community, since it facilitates interaction across schools and disciplines, can also create interdisciplinary learning opportunities. Finally, the local community is a democratic real-world learning site in which community members and academics can pragmatically determine whether the work is making a real difference and whether both the neighbourhood and the institution are better as a result of common efforts. A focus on local engagement is an extraordinarily promising strategy for realizing institutional mission and purpose. As elegantly expressed by Paul Pribbenow, president of Augsburg College, the "intersections of vocation and location" provide wonderful opportunities for both the institution and the community (Pribbenow 2014:158).

Conclusion and recommendations

This article has tried to provide the rationale for an anchor institution approach to advancing teaching and research and improving the quality of life in our local communities. We have provided a brief overview of institutional efforts to support the University of Pennsylvania's role as an anchor institution, dedicated to creating sustainable, democratic partnerships with its neighbours in West Philadelphia. It certainly remains, very much, a work in progress.

Increased faculty and student involvement through academically based community service and university-assisted community schools; the development of numerous sustained, democratic partnerships in the community; and the growing investment of institutional resources to support community economic development make it clear that we have come a long, long way. But there are miles and miles to go.

There are key lessons Penn has learned along its trajectory to realizing its role as an anchor institution. Support of institutional leadership — President, senior administrators, faculty — is key for infusing local engagement across campus, as well as to integrating engagement into the university's core academic mission and its mission of corporate citizenship. To sustain these efforts, organizational units need to be created or re-oriented. Methods of working need to change. The community must become a key partner working with the university on projects that are mutually determined and mutually beneficial. Finally, changing institutional culture and revitalizing communities takes time and ongoing, sustained partnerships as well as patience are essential.

An increased focus on local, democratic engagement is an extraordinarily promising strategy for realising institutional mission and purpose and improving the quality of life in some of our most vulnerable communities. "Only connect!" The powerful, evocative epigraph to E. M. Forster's *Howard's End* captures the essence of our argument – namely, that the necessary transformation of research universities is most likely to occur in the crucible of significant, serious, sustained engagement with local schools and communities (Forster 1911).

References

Benson, L, Harkavy, I., & Puckett, J. (2007) *Dewey's Dream: Universities and democracies in an age of education reform*. Philadelphia, PA: Temple University Press

Bok, D. (2003). *Universities in the marketplace: The Commercialization of higher education*. Princeton, N.J.: Princeton University Press.

Center for Educational Research and Innovation. (1982) *The University and the community: The problems of changing relationships*. Paris: Organisation for Economic Development and Development. pp. 1-167.

Davis, H. A., (2015), "Penn recognized for commitment to economic inclusion." Penn Current, July 2, 2015, available at https://penncurrent.upenn.edu/2015-07-02/latest-news/penn-recognized-commitment-economic-inclusion, accessed Jan 28, 2019.

Forster, E. M. (1911) *Howard's End*. Toronto: William Briggs.

Franklin, B. (1749/1962) "Proposals related to the education of youth in Pennsilvania [sic]", reprinted in Benjamin Franklin on Education, John Hardin Best (Ed.). New York, NY: Teachers College Press.

Harkavy, I. et al., (2009) "Anchor Institutions as partners in building successful communities and local economies" In P.C. Brophy and R. D. Godsil (Eds.), *Retooling HUD for a catalytic federal government: A report to Secretary Shaun Donovan*. Philadelphia: Penn Institute for Urban Research, pp. 147-169

Harkavy, I., Hartley, M., Hodges, R. A., Weeks, J. (2016) "The history and development of a partnership approach to improve schools, communities and universities" In H. Lawson and D. van Veen (Eds.) *Developing Community Schools, Community Learning Centers, Extended-Service Schools and Multi-service schools: International exemplars for practice, policy and research*. Cham, Switzerland: Springer International Publishing, pp. 303-321.

Johnston, F. E. & Harkavy, I. (2009) *The Obesity culture: Strategies for change: Public health and university-community partnerships*. Cambridge, U.K.: Smith-Gordon.

Office of the Executive Vice President, University of Pennsylvania. "Impact: University of Pennsylvania Powering Philadelphia and Pennsylvania (2015), Philadelphia: Office of the Executive Vice President, University of Pennsylvania, p 10. Available at: http://www.evp.upenn.edu/ pdf/ Penn_Economic_Impact_Powering_PHL_PA.pdf, accessed January 29, 2019.

Office of the Executive Vice President, University of Pennsylvania. "Penn's Economic Inclusion Initiatives," http://www.evp.upenn.edu/strategic-initiatives/community-and-economic-development/economic-inclusion-initiatives.html, accessed January 25, 2019.

Pribbenow, P. (Spring 2014) "Lessons on vocation and location: The saga of Augsburg College as urban settlement" Word and World 34, no 2, pp. 149-159. Available at: https://wordandworld.luthersem.edu/issues.aspx?article_id=3774, accessed January31, 2019.

Select Greater Philadelphia Council, (2016) "At the Heart of Good Business: Greater Philadelphia: The Place to Establish and Grow your Business," available at: http://selectgreaterphl.com/wp-content/uploads/2016/07/sgp16-report-select-report.pdf, accessed January 29, 2019.

The Pew Charitable Trusts. (2017) Philadelphia's poor: Who they are, where they live, and how that has changed. Available at: https://www.pewtrusts.org/en/research-and-analysis/reports/2017/11/philadelphias-poor, accessed January 29, 2019.

University City District. "West Philadelphia Skills Initiative: Results and impact" available at http://www.universitycity.org/impact, accessed January 29, 2019.

University of Pennsylvania Annual Report 1987-88: Penn and Philadelphia: Common Ground (p. 3), Philadelphia: Office of Publications Marketing Communications, University Relations, University of Pennsylvania.

University of Pennsylvania Financial Report 2008-2009 (p. 3). Philadelphia: Office of the Vice President for Finance and Treasurer, University of Pennsylvania.

CHAPTER 5
EMBEDDING ENGAGEMENT: THE EXAMPLE OF QUEEN'S UNIVERSITY BELFAST

Tony Gallagher

Introduction

Queen's College, Belfast was founded in 1845 as part of the federated Queen's University of Ireland, with constituent colleges in Belfast, Cork and Galway. Queen's University Belfast was granted independent degree-awarding powers in 1909 at a time when 'civic universities' were opening in many cities of the United Kingdom. In contrast to the 'ancient universities', all of which had been founded as ecclesiastical institutions in which academics were, quite literally, cloistered from the mundane concerns of day-to-day life, the civics were established with a commitment to their cities and regions. Most gave particular emphasis to applied science and technology, not least because they were generally founded in cities with significant industrial strength, and all saw for themselves a role in contributing to economic development as one of their core purposes.

With the partition of Ireland in 1922 – 23, and the establishment of Northern Ireland as a self-governing region within the United Kingdom, Queen's became a pillar of the Northern Ireland establishment. The 1947 Education Act (NI) provided access to free secondary education and presaged an expansion of higher education in the 1960s. The student body at Queen's hitherto had mainly been comprised of Presbyterians, but the 1960s saw an increase in the number of Catholic students, many of whom were influenced by a nascent Civil Rights campaign which challenged religious discrimination in Northern Ireland. On January 1, 1969, a group of about 70 young people, mainly Queen's students in a political group called People's Democracy, began a march from Belfast to Derry. This was inspired by the Selma to Montgomery march organized by Martin Luther King, but unlike it, the Belfast to Derry march was attacked by loyalist[1] protestors and received scant protection from the police. The

---

[1] The term 'loyalist' was applied to Protestant unionists who were militant in defence of keeping Northern Ireland in the United Kingdom. In 1969 the main leader of loyalists was Ian Paisley.

experience of the march was to put renewed energy into the Northern Ireland Civil Rights movement.

Towards an engaged university

This contrast between Queen's as an institution at the heart of the social, economic and political establishment in Northern Ireland, and at the same time the location for a campaign for radical change in Northern Irish society, was thrown into sharp relief by the onset of political violence in the Northern Irish Troubles[2] . Initially the former instinct prevailed, as research on the conflict was discouraged and Queen's tried to set itself apart from the chaos on the streets. This echoed a sentiment expressed some years previously by historians of Queen's who described it as a place where:

> '. . . within its walls the two communities have an opportunity of mingling in an atmosphere of freedom, equality, and mutual respect that they rarely find in any other sphere.' (Moody and Beckett 1959: 552)

This was a sentiment enshrined in official policy of the University in 1977 when the then Vice Chancellor, Professor Peter Froggatt, suggested that:

> 'Direct university involvement in society negates professional independence and jeopardizes the contract social [sic] that gives autonomy to the university in return for its institutional neutrality.' (Froggatt, 1977, cited in Taylor, 1988: 29)

The problem was that distance, in such contexts, never meant neutrality, but rather placed the institution, by default, on the side of authority. Such complacency as existed was challenged when a PhD study published by an English university claimed that there was a

---

[2] The political violence in Northern Ireland between 1968 and 1995 is euphemistically known as the 'Troubles'. Over 3,700 people died and many more were injured in violence involving the security forces, nationalist/republican paramilitaries and unionist/loyalist paramilitaries. The 'Troubles' ended with paramilitary ceasefires in 1995, the withdrawal of the British army from the region and a peace agreement in 1998.

significant under-representation of Catholics in the workforce at Queen's: using a variety of sources the study claimed that only five per cent of staff at Queen's in 1968 were Catholic, and only seven per cent were Catholic in 1982; by contrast it claimed that 27 per cent of staff were Protestant in 1968 and 39 per cent Protestant in 1982 (the remaining staff were identified as having come to Queen's from outside Northern Ireland) (Taylor, 1988). The response of the University to these claims when they received some media attention was terse:

> 'Queen's University does not keep any record of the religious affiliation of staff or students. We have no way of checking the claims made, nor do we intend to do so' (Osborne and Cormack, 1990: 332)

This complacency was shattered following a Fair Employment Agency (FEA) investigation into the University in 1992. The FEA had been created in 1972[3] as one of the reforms to address the challenges of the Civil Rights movement. The FEA was aimed at addressing religious and political discrimination in Northern Ireland, but had limited power beyond the capacity to carry out investigations into the religious composition of workforces. Employers were encouraged, but not required (until 1990), to monitor the composition of their workforces; and they were encouraged, but not required, to take action to improve any imbalances that might exist. The FEA report confirmed the under-representation of Catholics among employees at Queen's and criticized the university because:

> '… it had not monitored its own employment patterns, it had not reviewed the effectiveness of its recruitment procedures nor had it assessed the impact of its actions on the relative opportunities for employment offered to Protestants and Roman Catholics.' (Fair Employment Agency, 1989: 43)

---

[3] Originally it was established as the Fair Employment Agency. Its powers were significantly increased in 1989 when it was renamed the Fair Employment Commission. In the aftermath of the Good Friday Agreement it was merged with other agencies and was renamed the Equality Commission for Northern Ireland

In the wake of this, and a number of high-profile tribunal cases for which the University paid significant amounts in settlements, the University established an independent review of its own procedures, the conclusions of which were scathing:

> 'there has been 'a singular failure' at the highest levels to investigate allegations of inequality raised by the equal opportunities officer'. [The independent review made] 'more than 200 specific recommendations for changes in procedures ... a complete overhaul of employment practices to ensure equality.' (Independent, February 15, 1993[4])

These investigations did lead to a sea-change in recruitment procedures and the effects were dramatic: in 1991 Protestants comprised 60 per cent of the Queen's workforce and Catholics 20 per cent, but by 2015 this had changed to 37 per cent Protestant and 42 per cent Catholic[5]. This period was also marked by a growing level of research directly engaging with issues related to the conflict and division in Northern Ireland, and a more socially engaged approach generally by Queen's. One of the lessons of this may be that for universities to become more socially engaged requires more than a rhetorical commitment to engagement, but also a conscious and deliberate commitment to social inclusion, and equality in principle and in practice.

Queen's today

There is little doubt that Queen's University is now an engaged university, with an active and wide-ranging set of activities underpinning this work. Like many UK universities Queen's highlights its central role in the local Northern Ireland economy, through the direct and indirect contribution to employment, the supply of highly qualified graduates, the spending power of its staff and students, and its engagement with local business and industry. Queen's is a signatory

---

[4] https://www.independent.co.uk/news/uk/belfast-university-treats-catholic-staff-unfairly-1473071.html accessed January 11, 2019

[5] Figures derived from annual monitoring reports of the Fair Employment Commission, most of which can be access on the website of the Equality Commission Northern Ireland https://www.equalityni.org/Home accessed January 9, 2019

of the Manifesto for Public Engagement[6] which is promoted by the National Coordinating Centre for Public Engagement (NCCPE) and includes a commitment:

> … to sharing our knowledge, resources and skills with the public, and to listening to and learning from the expertise and insight of the different communities with which we engage.

Central to this Manifesto is the idea of partnership and co-creation with local communities, or publics. This represents the evolution of the approach to the generation and use of academic knowledge, from the days in which knowledge was generated in and for the university. Since then, the evolution can be described as making knowledge more accessible to people outside the university, to the point where there was an acknowledgement that communities outside the university had useful knowledge and they should be engaged with as partners, to the point where universities and communities co-create knowledge through the joint development of agendas and priorities. Furthermore, there is not only recognition that not all communities have the same level of access to, or engagement with, the University, there is also a recognition that engagement should pro-actively seek out connections with under-represented groups.

Queen's University has been moving along this path for considerable time now (Gallagher, 2013; Gallagher and Harrison, 2016; McDonald et al., 2016). More recently there has been an attempt to enhance this work and give it a strategic focus by creating a Social Charter[7]. The Social Charter made three main commitments:

- providing leadership, locally and globally
- promoting a positive impact on society through research and teaching
- promoting equality and social justice

---

[6] https://www.publicengagement.ac.uk/support-engagement/strategy-and-planning/manifesto-public-engagement accessed January 11, 2019
[7] https://www.qub.ac.uk/social-charter/, accessed January 9, 2019.

These over-arching commitments are realised through seven specific areas of activity, each of which has 'signature projects' which exemplify what the University is seeking to encourage and achieve.

Research with impact[8]

This is designed to encourage researchers to focus on projects with significant impact beyond the academic world, whether this is economic, social or cultural. Among the signature projects currently highlighted within this theme are projects which address, and seek to identify, ways to ameliorate, inequalities in access to cancer care across Europe; and work on shared education, which promotes collaborative networks between Protestant and Catholic schools in Northern Ireland and in other deeply divided societies. Each of these projects is based on high quality research, but the broader impact of the work is seen as central to their focus

Education with a social purpose[9]

This theme encourages the development of teaching and learning programmes which provide opportunities for students to engage with local communities for mutual benefit. Street society is an annual activity for Architecture students and staff in which they work with inner city communities to help them explore their built environment and identify ways in which it might be improved. Some years ago, the Queen's University Student's Union established a series of Homework Clubs through which student volunteers support pupils in non selective schools in areas which did not have a tradition of sending students to higher education. The first Club opened in a Protestant area close to Queen's, but there now exists a network across the city and students act as mentors for the young people.

The Science Shop, which cooperates with a parallel initiative in Ulster University, acts as a brokerage between community organisations and student projects: community organisations identify research projects they would like carried out and the Science Shop identifies students who could work on these projects as part of their degree programmes. The resulting project report is shared with the

---

[8] https://www.qub.ac.uk/social-charter/research-impact/, accessed January 9, 2019

[9] https://www.qub.ac.uk/social-charter/education-social-purpose/, accessed January 9, 2019.

community organisation which is free to use it in any lobbying activity it is carrying out. This initiative provides a mechanism in which students can get the opportunity to carry out research in real-life contexts, while the community organisations can access university expertise.

Breaking boundaries to produce new knowledge[10]

This theme is focused on encouraging innovation and creativity in tackling important global challenges. One example is provided by work on point of care diagnostic tests which aim to allow rapid, accurate diagnosis of serious bacterial infections in children. Research by the Institute for Global Food Security provided a means of measuring the level of inorganic arsenic in rice and is now focused on developing effective mitigation.

Equality and excellence[11]

Queen's' ambition is to support research that is globally excellent, while applying the results of that research for local benefit. A good example of this is provided by work on inner city education zones and, in particular, engagement with the Shankill community. This is a Protestant inner city area which suffers high levels of social deprivation and educational underachievement. It is an area which has suffered significant upheaval as a legacy of the political violence and urban regeneration. A very large number of short-term projects have been carried out in the community, over many years, but there was a growing frustration among community leaders that despite much activity, there was little evidence of real systemic change in the community. Several years ago the community decided to eschew short-term fixes in favour of a longer-term strategic approach that set out to change the life-chances of a new generation on the Shankill. The Centre for Evidence and Social Innovation (CESI) in Queen's has agreed to work with the community on this ambitious, long-term initiative: the partnership means that CESI provides expertise, evidence and experience on the effectiveness and design of interventions, while working with the community on long-term change processes. The fact

[10] https://www.qub.ac.uk/social-charter/breaking-boundaries/, accessed January 9, 2019

[11] https://www.qub.ac.uk/social-charter/equality-excellence/, accessed January 9, 2019

that this work is taken forward in partnership, and on the basis of a long-term commitment, is crucial.

A significant institutional contribution is provided by the Widening Participation Unit in Queen's which aims to expand social mobility and access to higher education. WPU runs junior and senior academies, focused on elementary and junior high school, and senior high school students respectively, in order to provide them with experience of the university environment. In addition there are specific programmes aimed at supporting mature students and young people who have been in care. In the 2019/20 academic year, an affirmative action scheme, the Pathway Opportunity Programme, is being launched: successful completion of the programme will lead to a reduced points offer for admission to one of a number of degree programmes in Queen's.

Civic culture and intercultural dialogue[12]
The aim of this theme is to provide opportunities for students to engage in dialogue and engagement to develop their sense of civic responsibility. One example is provided by SWOT, a student-led charitable medical society which raises money to provide medical equipment each year for developing countries. This is not simply a fund-raising activity, however, as the students undertake placements in the regions where the new equipment is located.

More generally, Queen's has provided an important forum for engagement with issues related to political conflict and conflict resolution, and has encouraged students to engage with the challenges of a post-violence society. Queen's has also acted as a venue for high-profile events that have encouraged reflection and consideration of anniversaries from the Troubles and their contemporary significance. One of the most significant was a major event to mark the 20th anniversary of the signing of the Good Friday Agreement in which former President Bill Clinton, and former Prime Ministers Tony Blair and Bertie Ahern participated[13] . Queen's also hosts a regular series of

[12] https://www.qub.ac.uk/social-charter/civic-culture-intercultural-dialogue/, accessed January 9, 2019
[13] https://www.qub.ac.uk/Research/GRI/mitchell-institute/good-friday-agreement-20-years-on/, accessed January 9, 2019

public lectures in which current political leaders are provided with an opportunity to engage with important policy issues[14] .

Sustainability[15]
Climate change and the priority of establishing new and sustainable means for energy production are not just research issues, but also are very concrete societal issues. Queen's runs a number of programmes which examine sustainable energy research and attempt to bridge the gap between industry needs and academic research, covering everything from hybrid buses to large-scale wave energy schemes. The CityZEN initiative[16] contributes to the European Union Smart Cities Programme to kick-start carbon descent in cities through direct design action.

Recognising and rewarding contributions from students and staff[17]
Support for initiatives under the Social Charter is encouraged by incorporating themes from it in the appraisal, promotion and rewards system for staff. The Students' Union has run a successful annual awards scheme to recognise student success and participation in entrepreneurship and volunteering. The University has established a Research Impact awards scheme further to encourage research projects which seek to promotes social, economic and cultural impact and make a positive difference on society. For students, the Degree Plus scheme has been in operation for many years to provide formal acknowledgement of student contribution and achievement beyond their degree programme while they were at the University and a Degree Plus certificate is awarded along with the Degree parchment which all students receive on graduation.

Conclusion
The case of Queen's University provides a useful example of ways in which a university can engage positively with its local city and region

---

[14] https://www.qub.ac.uk/public-engagement/Events/RobinSwannLecture.html, accessed January 9, 2019

[15] https://www.qub.ac.uk/social-charter/sustainability/, accessed January 9, 2019

[16] http://www.cityzen-smartcity.eu/home/about-city-zen/consortium/queens-university-of-belfast/, accessed January 11, 2019

[17] https://www.qub.ac.uk/social-charter/recognising-rewarding-contributions/, accessed January 9, 2019

and make a positive impact on society. The example highlights the importance of moving beyond a rhetoric of inclusion towards the practice of inclusion, but even then it helps if the institution make a formal commitment to engagement as a strategic priority. The development of the Social Charter is a clear attempt to do this, and it reflects the wide range of activities across the University which are encompassed within this priority area. The example of Queen's also highlights the fact that the role of a university changes over time, which is both a strength and a weakness: progressive gains can be reversed, and the challenges posed by Brexit and financial cutbacks risk driving institutional leadership to focus attention on traditional priorities, but the mainstreaming of engaged principles through the Social Charter, and in the reward and recognition system for staff and students, are all strengths. The main lesson of the Queen's University case, in other words, is not only the need to make a positive impact on society, but also to seek to embed this in practice.

References

Fair Employment Agency (1989): "Report of an Investigation into the Queen's University Section 12 of the Fair Employment (NI) Act 1976," (Belfast, FEA)

Gallagher, T (2013): "Student-community engagement at Queen's University Belfast", in S Bergan, I Harkavy & H van't Land (eds.), *Reimagining democratic societies: a new era of personal and social responsibility*. Strasbourg: Council of Europe Publishing Council of Europe Higher Education Series No. 18, pp. 247 - 53

Gallagher, T & Harrison, J (2016):" Civic engagement in a divided society: the role of Queen's University Belfast in Northern Ireland", in S Bergan, T Gallagher & I Harkavy (eds), *Higher education and democratic innovation*. Strasbourg: Council of Europe Publishing Council of Europe Higher Education Series, no. 21, pp. 51-62.

McDonald, J, Johnston, N, Busby, G with Gallagher, T (2016): "Community engagement in Belfast: Queen's University and the Sandy Row community", in S Bergan, T Gallagher & I Harkavy (eds), *Higher education for democratic innovation*. Strasbourg: Council of Europe Publishing Council of Europe Higher Education Series, no. 21,, pp. 63-70.

Moody, TW and Beckett, JC, (1959): *Queen's University 1845 to 1949 The History of a University (2 volumes)*, London: Faber and Faber

Osborne, RD and Cormack, RJ (1990): "Higher Education and Fair Employment in Northern Ireland", Higher Education Quarterly, 44(4), 325-343

Taylor, R. (1987) "The Limits of Liberalism: The Case of Queen's Academics and the Troubles", Politics, 7(2), 28-34

Taylor, R. (1988): "The Queen's University of Belfast: The Liberal University in a divided society". Higher Education Review, 20(2), 27-45

CHAPTER 6
WHEN YOUR LOCAL COMMUNITY IS SPREAD OUT:
THE UNIVERSITY OF THE AEGEAN

Spyros Syropoulos

Setting the Scene

The University of the Aegean is a public university with notable characteristics: not only it is peripheral; it is also insular, with campuses located in Lesvos, Chios, Samos, Rhodes, Syros and Lemnos - thus covering a very large and geo-politically sensitive area in the Eastern Mediterranean. It was founded on March 20, 1984, by Presidential Act 83/1984 and its administrative headquarters are located in the town of Mytilene, on the island of Lesvos. The university today comprises five Schools and 18 Departments offering undergraduate and post-graduate degree programmes. This growth was based on the administration's belief that its sustainability could only be based on its potential to grow into an institution of sufficient size to be sustainable, both in the number of Departments to support its study programmes and in the number of postgraduate courses to support its research. The premises of the University in Mytilene are located on a hill a few kilometres outside the city. Despite the universal acknowledgement of the importance of the university as a whole for the local community, I will concentrate on the example of the School of Humanities in the island of Rhodes (with the three Departments of Primary Education, Pre-school Education and Educational Design, and Mediterranean Studies). The School of Humanities is not only geographically central, since it is located in the heart of the city of Rhodes, but it has managed to become an inextricable part of local community life.

One could safely argue that all universities work on two levels: (a) academic excellence and (b) outward looking, internationalization - which is often considered (not without good reason) as a necessary prerequisite for the acknowledgement and recognition of excellence. There is, however, another level, often called the "third mission" of the university, i.e. the societal role of higher education institutions and their relationship with local communities.

Understandably, there are voices that argue for the detached character of universities. One could claim that universities are not public agents in the sense of institutions catering for the general social benefit and that they should not be interested, at least primarily, in this relationship, but that they should rather concentrate on promoting research, scientific knowledge and prioritize academic substance, instead of trying to prove themselves to the "audit society" (see argument in Bergan, 2011:168ff). Lately universities have been perceived as integral constituents of local communities, too, irremovable from within the society that surrounds them, affects them and is affected by them (Maurrasse, this volume). The relationship between local communities and higher education institutions is discussed by Henry Bienen, President Emeritus of Northwestern University in the US who describes it as a "town-gown" relationship:

> "It is to everyone's benefit to have and foster excellent "town-gown" relationships. But the town often believes not enough is being done and the gown often believes they are always in the town's crosshairs, where the town is always asking, "What can you do for me now?" no matter what has been done in the past".

> That said, town-gown relations are not inevitably poor. University leaders' participation in social and cultural events helps to foster these relationships. As such, inviting local political, religious and cultural leaders into the university is a good idea. Inviting town mayors, aldermen and alderwomen and other local leaders to sporting events, concerts and plays makes good sense. All of this relationship building helps to establish personal ties, which are immensely valuable in driving toward win-win situations between the town and the gown". (Bienen 2017).

Courant, McPherson and Resch have argued that the common US system of tiers in public higher education, with flagship universities, regional campuses, and community colleges, is economically efficient under plausible assumptions. They may be referring to higher education institutions in the U.S. but we may equally apply to the European experience their argument that: "many of the benefits of higher education adduced in this discussion - economic performance of graduates as well as overall economic productivity, citizenship, lower crime, etc. - are available by creating environments that are attractive to college graduates, but do not require producing college graduates locally. At the same time a number of considerations suggest an advantage to building rather than buying. These include the tailoring of research and training to local economic opportunities, the ability to compete for export income based on research and education, and such advantages as may accrue by providing educational opportunity to nearby residents, among others" (Courant, McPherson and Resch 2006: 303).

Town and gown

The "town-gown" relationship is a reciprocal one. Judging from the example of the cultivation of social integration of the School of Humanities in Rhodes, one could list a series of benefits for the university, such as:

- Gaining practical support (i.e. donation of municipally owned buildings to the university, financial support).
- Attracting undergraduate students from the local community.
- Attracting postgraduate students from the local community, with the notable examples of the Mayor of Rhodes and the Vice Governor of the region enrolled in Master's Courses at the School of Humanities in 2015 and 2017 respectively.
- Faith in the university and building a sense of "belonging".

Of course, one might also identify possible drawbacks from the effort to cultivate such a relationship. For example:

- The university loses its glory, its sense of awe. One could pose the issue of "too much proximity".
- Negative aspects of popularization of knowledge (one might argue that making scientific knowledge popular, diminishes its sense of awe and interest to those who might consider its "popular version" sufficient and might not develop an interest in taking it up as an area of academic study).

To manage and organize a Higher Education Institution requires the application of social and cultural strategies, so that its members feel affiliated to it as a community (Thoenig and Paradeise 2018). But this should not be the only concern of a higher education institution. A university as an institution and organization must be integrated in its wider, but also in its immediate, social environment. Today we are in position to acknowledge "the contribution of the university to the institutional capacity of the region through engagement of its management and members in local civil society (Goddard and Kempton 2011, section 1). The present author would also argue that the concept and degree of socialization of the institution can be assessed through certain functional features and indicators, such as: proof of academic excellence, measurable social ties, popularization of knowledge and investment in its relations with the local community. Let us examine them in detail, in relationship to the example of the School of Humanities in Rhodes.

Proof of academic excellence

Why should the university need to prove its academic excellence to the local community? Is it even possible for non-academics to comprehend it and appreciate fully the essence of academic excellence? Even if some members of the community may not be interested in the finer aspects of such terms and issues, what is at stake is the building of trust and faith in "our university's" distinction. The reputation of a university might affect students' choice (Minsky 2016), and it can also change the way that locals see it and respond to it.

One way to indicate excellence is university rankings. It remains questionable whether rankings actually say anything about the quality of an institution or its value to the local community or whether they only contribute to the "marketization" of specific institutions (Marginson, 2013; Stergiou and Tsikliras, 2014). For the present argument, rankings will be considered only as a means of showing to the local community aspects of the quality of the higher education institution that operates within its realm. The indication measuring of academic excellence to the local community could be achieved by disseminating the publicity of rankings which might not find their way to public attention otherwise. For example, the University of the Aegean was ranked for the first time in its history in 601st-800th range in the World University Rankings by *The Times Higher Education*[1] and it has been included in this list since. This was important for the university but it certainly could not have any effect on the local community which, as expected, was ignorant and indifferent to a point of information that might be of interest only to faculty and, perhaps, prospective students. However, when the news made it to the local as well as national press, through the public relations office of the University of the Aegean, the response of the readers of the local press was enormous. The announcement in the local press of the results of the External Evaluation Report of 2016 (Hellenic Quality Assurance and Accreditation Agency 2016)[2] played an even greater role. The external evaluation was organized by the Hellenic Quality Assurance and Accreditation Agency. The University of the Aegean has received as a total institutional rating, the highest predicted "Worthy of Merit", one of seven universities with the highest performance (University of the Aegean, University of Crete, School of Fine Arts, University, Aristotle University of Thessaloniki, Technical University of Crete, National and Kapodistrian University of Athens). In addition, the University of the Aegean received the highest overall rankings in the 26 sub-units, among all the universities in the country: 18 "Worthy of Merit", 7 "Positive", 1 "Partially Positive"[3] . The results were visible in the influx of students for the years to follow, the increase of students from the region and the greater response of people to various university events.

Measurable social ties

The building of social ties is not easy. The response to social problems demonstrates the social sensitivity of the University, thus reinforcing the sense of trust in and respect for its mission. The University of the Aegean responded rapidly to the burning issue of the increasing number or refugees over the past few years in Greece (for another example, from the US, see Murphy 2018; Kotsiou, et al. 2018). The university not only decided that a small percentage of the refugees, should they meet specific standards such as mastery of language and

---

[1] https://www.timeshighereducation.com/world-university-rankings/
university-aegean.. Accessed January 6, 2019.
[2] https://www.adip.gr/instevalreports/FINAL%20EXTERNAL%20
EVALUATION%20REPORT_UNIVERSITY%20OF%20THE%20AEGEAN.pdf.
Accessed January 6, 2019.
[3] https://www.adip.gr/en/insteval-reports.php, accessed January 12, 2019

proof of relevant academic background, be admitted in various departments[4], but it also participated in various actions with NGOs in the island of Mytilene. Mytilene, which received the biggest wave of the refugee influx in Greece, with discernible political and social effects (Wike, Stokes, Simmons 2016; Kalantzakos 2017: esp. p. 20). In Rhodes, the School of Humanities organized language courses for the refugees, public events for giving voice to refugees and specifically women refugees. Furthermore, members of the University of the Aegean, including the author of this article, participated as observers in the process of assessment for the European Qualifications Passport for Refugees[5], a project based on the Council of Europe/UNESCO Lisbon Recognition Convention[6] . The interest of the School of Humanities in issues of local social sensitivity include the School's participation in the blood donors campaign, with the organizing of one-day information events and conferences at the premises of the University, including the presence of mobile blood-collecting units. The results were encouraging since a great number of students became blood donors and donors of bone-marrow. This was considered extremely important since the region is, unfortunately, ranked first in Greece in terms of lethal car accidents.

Furthermore, the School of Humanities' faculty eagerly participate in local and regional administration. The academic expertise of university teachers of various academic backgrounds made them the logical and desirable choice for the boards of municipal committees such as the scientific board of the International Center of Writers and Translators of Rhodes, the Municipal Organization for Culture and Sports of Rhodes, the Regional Council of Research and Innovation, the regional Council of Antiquities and Monuments, etc. Notable events were co-organized by the UoA and the Municipality, such as "Freedom of Expression and Censorship", an international conference organized by the Department of Mediterranean Studies of the University of the Aegean and the municipal organization International Center of Writers

---

[4] University of the Aegean, Senate Decision of February 8, 2015.

[5] https://www.coe.int/en/web/education/recognition-of-refugees-qualifications, accessed 2 January 2019

[6] https://www.coe.int/en/web/conventions/full-list/-/conventions/treaty/165, accessed January 2, 2019.

and Translators of Rhodes (3-4 October 2014), under the auspices of UNESCO, with 25 speakers from 15 different countries[7].

Popularization of knowledge

The prime objective of each higher education institution is to produce and disseminate scientific knowledge, initially targeted to a specific group of immediately involved participants who constitute the academic community (although there is arguments for the right of anyone to enjoy this good, cf. Bergan 2011: 106). The knowledge and skills gained by this group is diffused in society through their incorporation into the professional and social fabric. So, the logical dilemma is whether there is any reason at all to consider possible advantages from making academic knowledge literally popular. Part of the answer lies in the fact that popularization of knowledge demonstrates that the university has become close to the community. People who were, in fact, unaware or ignorant of what the university actually does, what kind of knowledge and skills it produces and what its potential is, become not only aware, but also interested in the "local institution". This, in turn, enhances the sense of trust, as previously argued.

In order to achieve this, the School of Humanities organizes annually a series of so-called Open Lectures, held every second month. The lectures invite faculty to present a topic of their academic expertise to the general public. The constantly large and increasing number of participants shows the action is successful. Furthermore, faculty members visit schools lecturing pupils (both of primary and secondary education); they participate in television documentaries and productions, both national and international, regarding local history and mythology; they also literally open the premises of the institution to the local community. Events like open CARPA lessons, local and chess-championships for schools and other events organized by non academic organizations were held at the School of Humanities.[8] This

---

[7] http://www.tswtc.org/2014/10/04/freedom-of-expression-and-censorship-conference-rhodes-2nd-5th-of-october-2014/, accessed January 6, 2019

[8] For the use of the premises of the School of Humanities for the School Chess Championship, see: http://topika-nea.gr/index.php/epikairotita/16090. Accessed January 6, 2019. For the CARPA lessons and the use of Automatic External Defibrillator see https://www.rodiaki.gr/article/351411/. Accessed January 6, 2019.

puts the university at the heart of the community, leading people to consider it as something that belongs to all community, not only to an exclusive part of it.

Invest in sustainable development

The continuous growth and development of the university, both in economic and scientific terms, is related, even if not exclusively, to its strengthened relationship with its social and political environment. The School of Humanities has signed a Memorandum of Cooperation with the Municipality of Rhodes (2017), it co-organized the first National Conference on the Relation of Municipalities, Universities and Sustainable Development (2011) and today faculty of the School of Humanities participate in the Regional Council of Research and Innovation.

The results were visible in the fact that the "local" university is considered so important that it receives regional funding for activities like archaeological excavations on the island (for the faculty and students of the Department of Mediterranean Studies), municipal and regional financial support for conferences, the donation of buildings for the educational and administrative needs of the School, the renovation of the central building of the university with European funds through the Region of Southern Dodecanese in 2014 (11 million Euros) and the decision to invest 5 million Euros in the purchase of a hotel to cover accommodation needs for students.

To sum up, the relationship of the university with the local community is a reciprocal one. There are gives and takes for both sides. By reaching out to the community that surrounds it, the university gives knowledge, boosts the local economy (through the influx of a steady student population and jobs around it) and it offers an exceptional kind of status to the community. For example, when the city of Rhodes was a candidate for Cultural Capital of Europe for 2021, the fact that it was a "university city" figured prominently in its candidature. The inextricable interdependence of the four growth factors (Trust, Integration, Proximity, Sustainable Development) can be seen in the following scheme developed by the author:

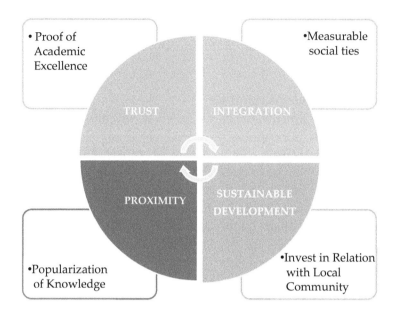

Popularization of Knowledge develops and is achieved through the proximity of the University to the local community; Proof of Academic Excellence builds Trust in the University on behalf of the local community; Measurable Social Ties lead to substantial Integration into the community; if the latter is followed by a carefully cultivated Investment in the relation with the local community it can achieve a substantial degree of Sustainable Development. Thought of in this way, higher education institutions become anchor-institutions, irremovable from their social, economic and geographical environment. They are not only dependent on their local communities, but also reflect and affect them in many ways, other than the strictly academic ones.

References

Bergan, S. (2011): *Not by bread alone*. (Strasbourg: Council of Europe Publishing. Council of Europe Higher Education Series No. 17.)

Bergan, S. and Harkavy, I. (eds). (2018): *Higher Education for Diversity, Social Inclusion and Community. A Democratic Imperative*. (Strasbourg: Council of Europe Publishing Council of Europe Higher Education Series No. 22)

Bienen, H. (2017): "The Role of Major Universities in their Local Communities". https://evolllution.com/revenue-streams/market_opportunities/the-role-of-major-universities-in-their-local-communities/. Accessed December 28, 2018.

Courant, P. N, McPherson, M., and Resch, A. M. (2006): "*The Public Role in Higher Education*", National Tax Journal, Vol. 59, No. 2 (June): 291-318.

Goddard, J. & Kempton, L. (2011): Connecting Universities to Regional Growth: A Practical Guide. A guide to help improve the contribution of universities to regional development, with a view to strengthening economic, social and territorial cohesion, in a sustainable way. Smart Specialisation Platform no. 3. European Union Regional Policy. https://ec.europa.eu/regional_policy /sources/docgener/presenta/universities2011/universities2011_en.pdf, accessed January 2, 2019.

Hellenic Quality Assurance and Accreditation Agency (2016): "External Evlaaution Report. University of the Aegean", available at http://www1.aegean.gr/aegean2/evaluation/UoAegean-External-Evaluation-Report-2016-EN.PDF, accessed 2 January 2019

Kalantzakos, S. (2017): "A Paradox in today's Europe? Greece's Response to the Syrian Refugee Crisis". The Jean Monnet Papers on Political Economy, no. 15. https://www.uop.gr/images/files/jeanmonnet_15.pdf, accessed January 2, 2019.

Kotsios, O., Kotsios, P., Srivastava, D., Kotsios, V., Gourgoulianis, K. & Exadaktylos, A. (2018): "Impact of the Refugee Crisis on the Greek Healthcare System: A long Road to Ithaca". In International Journal of Environmental Research and Public Health, Vol. 15, 1790.

Marginson, S. (2013): "University rankings in critical perspective", The Journal of Higher Education 84 (4):544-568.

Maurrasse, D. (this volume): "What Is an Anchor Institution and Why?"

Minsky, C. (2016) "What impact does university reputation have on students". https://www.timeshighereducation.com/student/news/what-impact-does-university-reputation-have-students. Accessed 20 December 2018.

Murphy, B. (2018): "Refugees, immigrants and migrants in higher education - The perspective of an open-access institution". In Bergan, S. & Harkavy, I. (eds). (2018): *Higher Education for Diversity, Social Inclusion and Community. A democratic Imperative.* (Strasbourg: Council of Europe Publishing Council of Europe Higher Education Series No. 22), pp. 131-141.

Stergiou, K. I & Tsikliras, A (2014) "Global university rankings uncovered: introduction", Ethics in Science and Environmental Politics, Vol. 13, pp. 59-64.

Thill, G. & Warrant, F. (1998): *Plaidoyer pour des universités citoyennes et responsables. Namur: Presses Universitaires de Namur* [the author used the Greek translation by E. Theodoropoulou & G. Xanthakou. (1999): 21 Athens: Atrapos].

Thoenig, J.-C. & Paradeise, C. (2018): " Higher Education Institutions as Strategic Actors ", in European Review, Vol. 26, No. S1, S57-S69.

Wike, R., Stokes, B. & Simmons, K. (2016): "Europeans Fear Wave of Refugees Will Mean More Terrorism, Fewer Jobs. Sharp ideological divides across EU on views about minorities, diversity and national identity". http://www.pewglobal.org/2016/07/11/europeans-fear-wave-of-refugees-will-mean-more-terrorism-fewer-jobs/. Accessed December 2, 2018.

CHAPTER 7
A TRADITIONAL UNIVERSITY IN ITS LOCAL COMMUNITY: THE JAGIELLONIAN UNIVERSITY IN KRAKÓW

Stanisław Kistryn

Introduction

Community engagement by higher education institutions should not be seen as a "philanthropic" activity, but as the main, or in fact the only mission of the universities. Often the institutional search for effective ways of developing and transmitting knowledge for the public good is referred to as "the third mission" of a modern university, as a supplement to its more widely recognized missions of educating students and performing scientific research. I am surely not alone in considering the last two to be only parts of a more general duty of any ambitious university of today – bringing up young generations in a knowledge-soaked environment, where the horizons of human understanding are advanced in many directions with care for the well-being of every single human.

That cannot happen without close contact with the university's surroundings – be it its town, its region, country or the whole world. Only combining the university's acquired knowledge with the community experience would allow it to address social disadvantages and promote the idea of a fair society. The university's services should be focused on issues and areas of paramount civic importance, such as sustainable development, improvement of public health, wider access to universal education, promotion of voluntary activity and development of citizenship.

From a societal point of view, community engagement is essential for public understanding and acceptance of research. The range of community engagement activities to be offered by researchers includes informing, consulting, involving, collaborating, and partnering with communities, and also contributing to citizen-led strategies. Let me summarize a few examples showing how we, at the Jagiellonian University in Kraków, try to fulfill our duties as a modern, socially embedded university.

The local community

The city of Kraków, apart from being a fabulous historical city in the Małopolska region (over centuries the capital of Poland and even today considered its cultural centre), is a vibrant job market and a city of many universities. It is not at all surprising that having trained highly qualified specialists in all kinds of fields, businesses are very frequently set up in our region. International investors establish branches of their corporations in the metropolitan area and offer students a multitude of opportunities to develop careers in their desired professions.

Research cooperation with local actors

As an emblematic element of the city and region, the Jagiellonian University makes an impact on the local community in many ways. Let me start with a central aspect of research – knowledge transfer. Local companies, especially small and medium enterprises, are the first, natural business partners for the Centre for Technology Transfer CITTRU, where inventions of academic scientists are offered for commercialization. Some of the companies acquire licenses from the Jagiellonian University as start-ups established by members of the academic community. As they grow, they create new jobs and influence the economic development of Kraków and the Małopolska region. To be more specific, let me just mention one example: MArCelLi Adv Tech, a technological start-up established in 2014 by Jagiellonian University employees with the participation of the EIT's Knowledge and Innovation Communities (KICs) and the AGH University of Science and Technology. The company is engaged in activities concerning the development and commercialization of electrode material manufacturing technology as well as electrolytes designed for applications in lithium-ion batteries (Li-ion), used in the Energy Storage Systems (ESS) and in electromobility (xEV). Close cooperation with the research units of both universities ensures the optimal access to their research infrastructure, new solutions and patented inventions.

The Jagiellonian University, through the Academic Business Incubator opened in 2015, helps young entrepreneurs (mostly students and researchers) to take their first steps in entrepreneurship, test their business models and survive the first, most crucial months of development. Such support is crucial for education and preparing students for their further professional career. The Incubator offers co-working space, trainings, seminars and consulting. It is worth mentioning that in 2017, the Incubator nurtured ten new start-ups.

Last but not least, various research teams from different faculties cooperate with the local surrounding, carrying out research on request, such as studies, analysis, research or reports for external entities. Delegating research work to an academic unit is an opportunity for fostering innovations for those companies that do not have their own R&D departments or that lack the appropriate equipment and expert knowledge, available at the Jagiellonian University. One of the Jagiellonian faculties that cooperates extensively with the business environment is the Faculty of Geography and Geology. Its scientists carry out regular hydrological research for ski resorts and for the national parks in the region. The research teams of the Faculty of Physics, Astronomy and Applied Computer Science developed an innovative solution, which refers to the protection of air quality: a network of monitoring stations equipped with sensors measuring the concentration of micro-particles in the air, temperature, humidity and pressure, which has already been installed in a few neighbouring municipalities.

Commissioned studies do not only refer to natural sciences. The Centre for the Evaluation and Analysis of Public Policies of the Jagiellonian University (CEAPP) specializes in tailor-made research and consultancy projects for public administration and non-governmental organizations. Both the Centre and the Department of Regional Geography (Faculty of Geography and Geology) often perform analyses and prepare reports for the local and regional authorities (the City of Kraków and the Małopolska Region Marshall's Office), having influence on the shape of their future social and economic policies.

Additionally, the Jagiellonian University is an owner of the Jagiellonian Centre of Innovation (JCI Ltd.), a company primarily responsible for managing the Life Science Technology Park and for providing a complementary set of services for entrepreneurs and scientists working in the field of life sciences: rental of specialized laboratories, financial support for innovative companies, contractual research and clinical trials and numerous educational initiatives. JCI is an example of creating infrastructure for science-business cooperation. The proximity of academic centres has significant influence on the performance of the high-tech companies in our region. They can benefit from the research conducted by the academic research units and by using highly qualified human capital trained by them. Another example of this close cooperation is the Life Science Cluster in Kraków, an initiative of Jagiellonian University established in 2006, bringing together 75 entrepreneurs, research institutions and hospitals.

Another example of a close collaboration between Jagiellonian University and the local authorities, supported by the EU funds, are projects led by the Jagiellonian Botanical Garden. They are devoted to the renovation of the historic greenhouses complex, containing unique palm tree species and an extensive collection of orchids and rare plants. These projects have received significant funds from the European Union, from the Regional Operation Programme for Małopolska region 2014-2020, measure 6.2: Protection of biological diversity.

Improving the effectiveness of the teaching process by employing modern technologies goes in parallel with care for the environment, by utilizing pioneering technologies in building construction and techniques of the management systems. The new premises of the Faculty of Chemistry, opened in September 2018, were designed and built with special attention to the natural environment, especially energy saving solutions and waste generation control. Due to the close cooperation with the Małopolska Regional Government, the Jagiellonian University philological sciences complex has been equipped with high-tech audio-visual and multimedia systems, as well as creating classrooms and working spaces taking into account the needs of students with various kinds of disabilities, thus paving the way for such solutions in other institutions.

A small scale example, but worth mentioning due to its environmental outreach, is the Jagiellonian University Apiary, which was opened at the University Botanical Garden at the beginning of summer 2017. Since then, the University has collaborated with a local Kraków apiary to provide the required education to beginner beekeepers to enable them to produce honey and join the bee protection initiative. The University Apiary has been our response to the growing trend of urban beekeeping and bee protection. The Kraków parks and commons are an ideal environment for these industrious insects. Although beekeeping becomes increasingly difficult due to disease, pesticide use, and invasive bee species, the city's green areas offer easy access to well-fertilized plants that produce plenty of nectar. Because of this, urban apiaries yield clean, nutritious honey. And at the same time urban apiaries illustrate to the public the importance of preserving indigenous elements of human environment.

The Jagiellonian University also started a new project funded by the Operational Programme Infrastructure and Environment 2014 - 2020, destined for the Trauma Centre of the University Children's Hospital. This EU grant will support the purchase of new equipment (i.e. MRI apparatus and two ultrasonic machines, three cardiac monitors and a defibrillator) that will help save the lives of children who have suffered multiple organ damage. The Trauma Centre, planned to open in 2019, is another important step in the hospital's development in our region. That project is an indication of numerous activities of the medical section of the university, always at the frontline of helping people suffering from various diseases.

Conclusion and future developments
A university, by its very nature, cannot be local only. Or rather – for a good and ambitious university engagement is both local and global and the two cannot easily be separated. By developing contacts with very different cultures and societies, the university contributes to openness, tolerance and the appreciation of universal, democratic, human values. Jagiellonian University is one of the leading Polish research institutions with well-developed collaboration with major academic centres from all over the world. The most important large-scale projects run by the University include the Jagiellonian Centre for Experimental Therapeutics, the Małopolska Centre for Biotechnology, the Molecular Biotechnology for Health and the National Synchrotron Radiation Centre "Solaris." All those infrastructures attract scientists from various parts of the world, are elements of wide international networks of similar laboratories and thus contribute to creating a knowledge-oriented and knowledge-based society. For a long time, the Jagiellonian University has been involved in various international research programmes, such as the Sixth and the Seventh Framework Programmes and Horizon 2020 as well as numerous international university networks. Such comprehensive cooperation, together with business and local communities support, is a significant factor in shaping effective university management methods as well as improving the teaching process.

I am aware, however, that there is still a lot to do in this field. Despite some recent substantial changes in the higher education sector, including the Jagiellonian University's engagement in fostering and improving its cooperation, especially with local communities and business, many types of initiatives existing in other countries are still not popular in the Polish academic landscape. Hardly ever seen are education initiatives, such as university-assisted community schools, programmes concerning community development or training for community-based organizations. Community partnerships should also involve awarding grants for community development at minority serving or community-oriented institutions. Meeting community needs means that more community research centres should be established and community-aimed scholarly work should be better recognized and rewarded. We need a profound change – across academic programmes, research and business practices – to improve the impact of academic work on the society. But I am optimistic that we are moving in the right direction.

CHAPTER 8
THE UNIVERSITY OF ICELAND'S PARTICIPATION IN THE LOCAL AND NATIONAL COMMUNITY: INCREASING IMPACT, WIDENING ACCESS

Steinunn Gestsdóttir

Introduction

The University of Iceland (UI) plays a key role in the development of Iceland as a knowledge-based society. It is the country's leading scientific institution, the largest provider of higher education in Iceland, and the country's only international, comprehensive university. UI is located in the capital Reykjavík and comprises five schools, each representing broad academic fields: education, health, humanities, engineering and natural sciences, and social sciences. Indicative of UI's leading national role, it is home to approximately 13,000 students, or two thirds of the entire higher education student population in Iceland, including three of every four students at the Master's and 97% at Doctorate level. Its strength as an international research university is evidenced by its position among the top 300 research universities in the world. UI is also an active participant in industry and society, closely collaborating with all key Icelandic institutions, including ministries and parliament, and conducting several hundred collaborative projects between academic units and industry at any given time. Given UI's leading position in Iceland, it seeks to serve the Icelandic community, both at the local level in the capital Reykjavík, as well as at the national level.

In the current strategy for the university, for 2016-2021, active participation in society and the economy is one of the three main pillars. Consequently, one of the main goals of the strategy is to ensure that the work of the university has a wide impact on society and that it addresses the challenges of the 21st century. To this end, the strategy outlines several steps to ensure wide access to education, to identify how expert knowledge at UI can better benefit the community, and to inspire diverse collaborations with economy and the community, as will be described in this chapter.

In addition, and a major focus of this chapter, the strategy[1] outlines how UI can become an even more active participant at the local and national level, including the use of diverse science media to promote interest in and understanding of science, and foster productive collaboration and communication with earlier school levels.

Education that serves society: Widening access

In recent years, UI has launched a number of education initiatives to better serve wider society in Iceland, with an emphasis on widening access to the University and better serving students living outside of the capital. These include the development of recent professional education programmes (Icelandic: fagh*á*skólanám), renewed emphasis on blended learning and distance learning, design of massive open online courses (MOOCS), and a special vocational diploma programme designed for students with intellectual disabilities.

Professional education programmes are being developed at UI in early childhood education, health information science, applied engineering, and tourism studies. These initiatives aim to provide professional university training to a diverse group of students that do not meet the official entrance requirement (i.e. do not have the type of secondary school diploma required for admission). The programmes are especially designed to address the needs for certain professionals as defined by either professionals or public authorities and to provide access to UI for people with extensive working experience in their field. In developing the professional programme in early childhood education, for example, UI worked with local communities in South Iceland to provide much needed educational opportunities for individuals who have extensive experience working with children at preschools but have not received professional university training.

MOOCS and distance learning. UI is actively using diverse digital technologies to make education more accessible to students in Iceland and around the world. For example, UI became a charter member of edX-network, founded by MIT and Harvard in 2012 to provide high

---

[1] Strategy of The University of Iceland 2016-2021. https://english.hi.is/university/strategy_of_the_university_of_iceland_2016_2021, accessed on January 22, 2019.

quality MOOCS. UI's first edX-MOOC, Medieval Icelandic Sagas[2], was launched in 2018. Nearly 6,000 students from 113 countries have participated in this course, ranging in age from 13 to 82. Among the MOOCS currently being created at UI are courses on volcano monitoring, sustainable development in Iceland, intercultural competences, mathematics for incoming students at the University, and sheep grazing (in collaboration with the Agricultural University of Iceland and others).

Furthermore, in order to better meet students' changing needs, as well as to better serve working people and the communities beyond the capital Reykjavík, the university is in the process of renewing its emphasis on blended and distance learning by forming a new strategy on distance learning, selecting a new learning management system (LMS), and increasing support for academic staff in developing blended classes.

Finally, _the vocational diploma programme_ at UI is a part-time two-year inclusive vocational diploma programme for students with intellectual disabilities who have completed at least some upper secondary school education, but may not meet the official entrance requirement of the UI. The aim of the programme is to give the students an opportunity to pursue education and practical skills in an inclusive higher education setting in order to support their participation in society. Students comprise a diverse group; while some have been identified by health professionals as having "mild/moderate" disabilities, others' needs have been assessed as "severe". Since 2007, several dozens of students have graduated from the programme. It does not provide a university degree or access to further education, but aims at prepare students for specific jobs within the field of education, in pre-primary schools, after-school programmes, and within the field of disability and self-advocacy. In addition, the programme is one step towards increasing access and visibility of people with intellectual disabilities to all aspects of society, including institutions of higher education.

---

[2] University of Iceland. _edX course The Medieval Icelandic Sagas._ https://www.edx.org/course/medieval-icelandic-sagas-uicelandx-uoi001x, accessed on January 22, 2019.

Active collaboration with economic actors and the application of research

The university wants to take a proactive role in its community by ensuring that the university's work, especially its research output, has a wide societal impact. Hence, UI is taking steps to further develop as an active forum for new ideas generated in collaboration with its community and encourage dynamic collaborations between researchers and economy and society. UI has several communication mechanisms to this end, including the on campus Science Park, the Technology and Knowledge Transfer Office, research centres across the country, and support of collaborations with economy and community.

The University of Iceland Science Park is in the early phases of development. The project is in line with the entrepreneurial university and the triple helix model of innovation (Steinthorsson, Hilmarsson & Janusson 2017). The City of Reykjavik is the university's main partner in this project along with selected innovative companies in the fields of genetics, pharmaceutical development, and IT and gaming. The Science Park is a community on campus where scientists bring their ideas and discoveries to the table and, in collaboration with students and industry, convert them into applied knowledge and commercial products. The Science Park is an enthusiastic, supportive community for academia and research-based companies. The challenge is to create an innovative environment that attracts experts from both sides to foster ideas and develop them into exciting and successful business opportunities.

TTO Iceland is a UI initiative and serves as a Technology and Knowledge Transfer Office for all universities and leading research organizations in the country[3] . TTO Iceland identifies and supports innovative research projects, provides protection for intellectual property, and communicates projects to industry and investors in Iceland and abroad. One of the purposes of TTO Iceland is to increase economic growth, productivity and the country's competitiveness, and the positive social and environmental impact of scientific work in Iceland.

---

[3] See https://ttoiceland.hi.is/english/, accessed January 29, 2019.

Regional research centres in rural areas. In the past two decades, UI has created nine regional research centres across Iceland (outside of the capital, Reykjavík) that work in close cooperation with the local municipalities, institutions, businesses, non-governmental organisation, and individuals. The research centres focus on issues that are specific to the local communities in question, such as whaling, earthquakes, national parks, history and folklore. As these centres have grown, they have proven to be important in promoting the creation of jobs in rural areas that require academic qualifications and in creating knowledge and value, which benefit these communities and wider society.

Systematic support of collaborations with economy and community. Finally, UI is currently assessing the evaluation and reward system for academic work to better support and acknowledge societal participation, collaboration, and outreach by academic staff. Again, consistent with UI's strategy, it is a vital step to acknowledge important contributions in this respect and to better support research addressing the challenges of the 21st century.

Public engagement

The University of Iceland puts great emphasis on providing platforms to deliver academic knowledge to the public and raising public interest in and understanding of science. This mission is prominent in UI's current strategy and can be divided into three parts: knowledge communication to the public, student volunteer programs, and outreach programs for children and youth.

Knowledge for the public

The university is highly committed to making the expertise and knowledge within UI available to the public, presented in a way that can contribute to the development of Icelandic society.

The Web of Science[4] (https://www.visindavefur.is, in Icelandic; see an abbreviated English version www.ask.is) is one of UI's most successful public outreach programs. It was launched in 2000 and is one of the

---

[4] https://www.visindavefur.is, in Icelandic; see an abbreviated English version www.ask.is, both accessed January 29, 2019.

most popular web portals in Iceland. It is a website where the public can send in questions relating to all fields of research, from astronomy to manuscript studies, from molecular biology to psychology, and receive answers from experts among the university staff. Visitors to the website can then read answers to previous questions and submit new questions. The questions go straight to academic experts. The Web of Science received roughly 2.1 million visits in the year 2018 and over 1500 questions, which means that roughly four questions were sent in each day in 2018. About 40 per cent of the questions received in 2018 have been answered.

University in Society. UI's most recent outreach programme is an annual series of lectures called University in Society. Each lecture series is focused on a societal issue that has been highly visible in public discourse. The first series pertained to the welfare of children and youth. A wide range of subjects were addressed, including anxiety and psychological health, how to support literacy, ways to promote children's participation in sports and out-of-school activities, the effects of nutrition and sleep for healthy functioning, and the role of parenting and positive communications in children's development. Experts within UI provided an overview of each issue with a focus on practical information for the public and professionals. In this way, the University aims to ensure that the expertise of academic staff can be used to support Icelandic families and society, as well as increase the public's trust in the university and create awareness of the diverse scientific work that it conducts. To ensure wide participation, each lecture was streamed online, made available via UI's website, and accompanied by videos where the lecturers give a short summery of the topic. In addition, presenters were featured in the general media for the week of the lecture. The lectures, and other materials, have been a great success; turnout and views exceeded expectations, making the series a very promising step in bringing scientific knowledge and expert advice to a wide audience.

TV programming. The Treasure of the Future is a TV series from UI that has been successful in attracting public attention towards research. The series sheds light on diverse and dynamic research carried out by scientists at the University of Iceland in varied circumstances. The episodes present research from all of UI's five Schools, with special emphasis on Icelandic natural resources such as renewable energy, fish stocks, sustainability, sustainable development, the ocean, the wilderness, volcanos and natural risks and disasters, as well as social issues such as immigration and crime and punishment, cancer treatments, and climate change.

Student volunteer programmes

One of the most valuable ways in which UI can support local communities is via the efforts of its students. The university offers a variety of outreach programmes in the society that have been developed, managed, and implemented by students, often with the support of academic staff. Student community projects involve a variety of topics, as listed below.

Astradur is programme run by medical students with the purpose of preventing sexually transmitted diseases (STD) and premature pregnancy. Medical students visit secondary schools and educate adolescents and young people about STDs, contraception, and abortion.

Another programme organized and run by medical students is *Bjargradur,* a first-aid education programme, which focuses on visiting upper secondary schools to teach students the basics of first-aid.

Skjoldur, a preventive educational programme run by students in nursing, offers education in elementary schools on self-image and the importance of good self-esteem. The goal of the programme is to provide prevention and education to youth, as well as enhancing the knowledge and skills of nursing students in issues of public health and strengthen their knowledge of evidence-based prevention methods.

The Hospital for Teddy Bears is also a medical students' initiative, where children aged between 3 and 6 years are given the opportunity to visit a hospital once a year with their sick or injured teddy bears. The aim of the project is to prevent children from being afraid of health professionals and hospitals, and to give medical students the opportunity to practice communication with children.

Orator, the union of law students, offers the public legal advice through telephone interviews, free of charge. The service is available during each school semester and is offered by graduate students of law under the supervision of practicing attorneys.

Psychological Counselling for university students is a training unit in clinical psychology, operated by the Faculty of Psychology. The aim is twofold: to train graduate psychology students in clinical counselling and to offer university students and their children psychological counselling services. The service is offered by students in clinical psychology under the supervision of practicing psychologists.

The Faculty of Odontology offers *dental services to the public*. The service is offered during the academic year. The main aims of the service are to train dentistry students and provide affordable services to the public.

Hugrun is an educational unit with the purpose of educating young people about mental health and available treatments and services, as well as contributing to better awareness about the importance of mental health. Hugrun is a collaboration of students in medicine, nursing and psychology.

Outreach programmes for children and youth
For over two decades the University of Iceland has worked to get young Icelanders engaged in science. In designing these initiatives emphasis has been placed on reaching students in rural areas.

University of Youth and the Knowledge Train. In the University of Youth local young people are invited to study at UI for one week of the summer. Youth aged 12 to 16 years are offered short courses in a variety of subjects, ranging from the human cell, nutrition, whales and insects, engineering, geology, designing a race car, political science, to Chinese and Japanese, taught by professors and graduate students at UI.

The Knowledge Train takes the concept of the University of Youth on the road. Staff travel to four locations across Iceland and offers up to ten free courses, selected from the University of Youth, in a local school. Students can choose and attend up to three courses over a one-day period. The courses are followed by a "Science Day" that is open to the public, which includes a planetarium, demonstration experiments, and more educational activates. Visits from the Knowledge Train are prepared in close collaboration with municipalities and primary schools in the local areas.

UI Science Centres is a popular outreach programme located on campus. The goal is to increase children's interest in the sciences through interactive and hands-on teaching and projects, simultaneously strengthen teaching in the field of the natural and physical sciences. The Science Centre is open to school groups free of charge and intended for students in grades 6 through 10. The staff and instructors of the Science Centre are University of Iceland staff and students.

Conclusion

This chapter has described how social responsibility and community collaboration is manifested in UI's strategy and how multiple programmes have been developed to help fulfil this mission. As the leading educational and scientific institution in Iceland, UI has a great responsibility to constantly rethink its relations to society and actively seek new ways to positively impact the community at the local and the national level. In light of the growing and complex challenges facing communities in Iceland and across the globe, UI is committed to strengthening its commitment to having a meaningful impact at the local, national, and international level.

References

Steinthorsson, R. S., Hilmarsson, E. & Janusson, H. B. (2017). "Towards openness and inclusiveness: The evolution of a science park". Industry and Higher Education, 31 (6): 388-398.

CHAPTER 9
CAN INTERNATIONAL UNIVERSITIES BE ANCHOR INSTITUTIONS? LOCAL, REGIONAL, AND GLOBAL: THE CENTRAL EUROPEAN UNIVERSITY

Liviu Matei

Introduction

This chapter looks at the case of the Central European University (CEU), a higher education institution that is "densely international" and "international by design" (Matei 2008). Can international universities be anchor institutions? The analysis of this particular case shows that the answer is positive: international universities can successfully combine local, regional and global ambitions in their missions and activities. They can be anchor institutions, although perhaps not exactly in the same ways as their peers with an exclusive or primarily local mission. The chapter proposes to expand and refine the meaning of "anchor institution", taking into account the experience of international universities, of the CEU in this case. It puts forward elements for a new definition, looking at distinctive characteristics of international universities as anchor institutions.

The concept of anchor institution and the place of international universities

The concept of anchor institution is relatively new in the scholarship of public policy and higher education, if not in the practice of higher education institutions. It originates in the United States, where it was first promoted by a handful of institutions, scholars and practitioners (Maurrasse 2001 and this volume; Ehlenz 2018). The creation of the Anchor Institutions Task Force (AITF) in the US in 2009, with a large membership, has contributed significantly to promoting this approach and giving the concept visibility[1] . In Europe, it is a very recent addition to the higher education policy debate and the term is rarely used. It is

---

[1] The Task Force has sponsored many events and publications since its establishment. It maintains a very useful website: https://www.margainc.com/aitf/, accessed February 25, 2019.

unclear whether even a single European university to date identifies itself as an anchor institution, although quite a few undertake activities and have results that would justify using this label (Smith 2018). European concepts and initiatives, such as that of civic university or smart specializations (Fotakis et al. 2014; Smallbone et al. 2015; Smith 2018) come very close to the US concept of anchor institution or may even be identical.

"Anchor institution" is a relatively precise concept. It emphasizes the commitment to working systematically with the local authorities and especially with local communities, even to build local communities, to help "anchor" people, organizations, businesses, other economic, social and cultural activities around given places. The existing literature on this subject indicates that anchor institutions, when successful, make important contributions to their surrounding neighbourhoods and communities, in particular through economic and social revitalization, urban redevelopment and improving the delivery of city services and the welfare of urban residents (Goodman 2014). One of the best-known examples, a real prototype, is Rutgers University in Newark, (RU-N), which openly defines itself as an anchor institution, with a mission, strategic planning, organization and activities that are explicitly geared towards and supportive of this profile:

> "Rutgers ... is a remarkably diverse, urban, public research university that is not just in Newark but of Newark—an anchor of our home city. ... our location is both a defining influence in our story and a distinctive strength. ... Our campus recently completed a strategic visioning process that underscored this defining aspect of RU-N's identity, yielding a strategic plan that emphasizes the need to develop even more fully and purposefully our anchor institution agenda. ... Our goal is to move away from traditional models of "public service" in which faculty and students do things for "a passive and needy public," ... and engage instead in "public work that taps and engages and develops the civic agency, talents, and capacities of everyone, inside and outside the academy."[2]

---

[2] https://www.newark.rutgers.edu/anchor-institution, accessed February 25, 2018.

Like Rutgers, successful anchor institutions concentrate on a particular community to promote initiatives based on their academic and professional assets (fundamentally, based on knowledge) to promote better health, economic development, safety, education, employment or simply a better quality of life for the members of those communities or neighbourhoods. When anchor institutions work well, they work closely with their communities and are appreciated and supported by these communities, which become not just passive beneficiaries, but active participants. Universities, in turn, become "members" of those communities in some way. They anchor themselves explicitly and strongly around that given place or "locality".

We may ask what happens when an institution aspiring to be an anchor is not "local," by virtue of its demography (students, faculty and staff) or mission. What happens when a large majority of students does not come from the city or region in which the institution is located, but from the outside, even from faraway countries? Is it still possible to be an anchor institution? Is it reasonable even to think about being an anchor when the mission of the institution and its constituency are not local or even regional, but rather international and eventually global? What do local communities think about international universities operating in their midst?

Many international universities do work with their surrounding communities as well. Moreover, some of them aspire to be anchor universities, while preserving their international profile and mission. The Central European University (CEU) is a good illustration.

The Central European University: international by design and a genuine anchor institution

The CEU has a very special, even unique, institutional profile, mission, organization and demography. Although it does not define itself formally as an anchor institution, the CEU is one, in ways that reflect its particularities.

A mission-driven university with a special institutional profile

The CEU was established in 1991, after the fall of the Berlin Wall, at the initiative of dissidents from the former communist countries of Central and Eastern Europe (CEE). The founding group included Václav Havel, the well-known Czech intellectual and politician, the first post-communist president of Czechoslovakia and the first president of the Czech Republic; Bronisław Geremek, a former leader of the Solidarity trade union in Poland, celebrated medieval studies scholar and important Polish and European politician in the post-communist period; and Miklos Vasarhelyi, a prominent Hungarian intellectual in the second half of the 20th century and one of the leaders of the 1956 anti-communist revolution in Hungary. Together with George Soros, a visionary philanthropist and thinker of Hungarian origin, they decided to create a university dedicated to the study and promotion of open society and democracy through advanced research, graduate teaching and learning (no undergraduate programmes were envisaged) and civic commitment. Moreover, they decided that this university should serve an entire region, Central and Eastern Europe (CEE), rather than a particular city, sub-region, or country.

As a consequence, unlike most other universities of our time, the CEU is not internationalizing. It was born international - it is international by design (Matei 2008). All of its 1500 students currently enrolled in master and doctoral programmes are international students, by now coming not only from the CEE region but are recruited from about 160 countries. Operating in Budapest, the CEU enrols about 250 Hungarian students, the largest single national group, but representing only a small minority of less than 20% of the total student body. Although studying in their own country, given the overall demography, intellectual agenda and pedagogic model of the CEU, they are *de facto* international students, treated as such and exposed to an international student experience. There is no International Student Office at CEU because every single student is an international student, even the local, Hungarian students. Faculty and staff members come from 40 countries. The CEU is resolutely international. In some classes, also given their small size (12 on average), there are not even two students from the same country. Unlike at other universities that have many international students and from even more countries, at the CEU there is no national majority.

The CEU's intellectual agenda is not national - it is regional and international. The CEU promotes research and education that is largely comparative in character, focusing on Central and Eastern Europe as a whole and, increasingly, taking a global perspective in the pursuit of critical inquiry into issues, values and practices that are relevant to an open society.

The CEU started in Prague in 1991. It was forced to move to Budapest in 1995 when the then- prime minister argued against letting an international university and "alien students" use a building that was a "national Czech asset". Currently, the CEU is in the process of moving once again to another country, this time to Austria, having been chased out of Hungary by the repressive, nationalist and anti-intellectual regime of Viktor Orban[3] .

The CEU is a research-intensive, international university dedicated to a broad regional/international constituency and with ambitions of being of service globally, under the auspices of open society and democracy. The language of instruction is English. Students spend a year or two in Budapest in master programmes and four to six years for a doctorate. Eighty per cent of them will return to their countries of origin after graduation, while the others will pursue careers in other countries. The number of non-Hungarians who settle in Hungary is insignificant.

How can such a non-local, non-national university be an anchor? An anchor for whom? And how?

An anchor institution at the local, regional, international and global level

The CEU has the capacity to act as an anchor institution not only at the local level, more or less in accordance with the by now conventional meaning of the concept, but also, if we use an expanded understanding of the term, at the national, regional, international and possibly even global level. This is possible given the CEU's ambition to act as an

---

[3] "At the end of March 2017, a set of amendments to the National Higher Education Law were passed by the Parliament of Hungary. The passage of the bill required an unprecedented expedited procedure imposed by the government. To protest both the content of the bill and the unapologetically aggressive manner in which it was passed, some 70,000 people took to the streets of Budapest on April 7, 2017, in one of the largest mass actions in Hungarian history. Despite the protests, Hungarian President János Áder signed the bill into law three days later. The action led to an immediate outcry from academics and non-academics in Hungary and abroad, who charge that it represents a brutal attack against academic freedom and institutional autonomy. The new law is perceived by many as targeting one international higher education institution in particular: Central European University. Critics of the legislation even refer to it as "Lex CEU" to emphasize just how draconian its attack on a single institution is." (Matei and Orosz 2017)

institution that - through research, teaching and learning, and civic commitment - helps formulate, put on the public agenda. and address major problems of definite communities that represent its constituencies.

I propose that the ambition and capacity, to identify, formulate, put on the public agenda. and help address major challenges of clearly circumscribed communities be understood as an intrinsic, perhaps even the core, element of the definition of an anchor institution.

We will review briefly a few selected examples for the case of the CEU, on each level (local, national, regional, international, global), looking in every case at the exact community "anchored", the needs that the CEU helped identify and put on the public agenda, and the action taken to address them.

Local

Urban redevelopment Budapest

Having lost its original premises in Prague, the CEU moved fully to Budapest in 1995. Since then it has operated in a downtown complex of classic buildings in or near a UNESCO-protected area, some of which it owns, while the others are rented from local authorities and private owners. The CEU undertook waves of redevelopment of its premises, in cooperation with its neighbours and the authorities. Like many other universities, the CEU used such projects as an opportunity to engage not only in architectural refurbishment but in urban redevelopment as well. The last redevelopment project had to be halted in 2017 as a consequence of political attacks on the CEU by the Hungarian government. That project has nevertheless produced iconic buildings, already recognized as such in Hungary and abroad. As a rule, these buildings include public-use functions and areas. The CEU organizes on a weekly basis, at least, well attended public events open to the broader Budapest public, with a business, civic, cultural, educational or scientific scope. People in the downtown neighbourhood appreciate the CEU's presence and activities. When the crisis generated by the adoption by the Hungarian Parliament of "Lex CEU" erupted in 2017, many of them expressed their solidarity and support. Many local businesses put the sticker with #IstandwithCEU in their windows to express their solidarity. One of the most moving gestures was when a local coffee shop in CEU's vicinity started to sell cappuccino with this hashtag written in English and Hungarian with cocoa powder on the foam of every cup they served to their clients.

Urban redevelopment Vienna

The adoption of "Lex CEU" forced the CEU to close down or move to another country (Matei and Orosz 2017). The CEU has chosen to move to Vienna, answering an invitation by the Viennese city and state authorities. Vienna offered the CEU historic premises - several pavilions and adjacent buildings in a large, beautiful park on the outskirts of the city, all designed by a famous architect and built in 1907. The hospital currently on the site is being decommissioned and the city does not have the funds to redevelop the site. Residents of the neighbourhood protested strongly when the city started looking for commercial development solutions and persuaded the city government to sign an agreement stating that the use of the site will be restricted to cultural and educational purposes. There is no non-commercial tenant other than the CEU that has the interest and the means to redevelop this large and expensive site, which also has a controversial history going back to the Nazi occupation and pre-Second World War period. Both the city and the neighbours, as well as other Viennese universities, are now pleased with the plan that the CEU will redevelop the site, move there and create facilities for the general public (a theatre) and for other Viennese universities (joint labs and an inter-university cultural centre). There is a broad consensus in Vienna that the CEU will bring unique academic and professional strengths in the social sciences and humanities and a student body and faculty that are unprecedented in their internationality. The planned contribution in terms of urban redevelopment is no less appreciated.

Library services

The CEU has the best library of social sciences in the entire Central and Eastern European region. Many of the CEU's library resources are unique in this part of the world. As a research-intensive university, all CEU students and faculty, and many members of the staff, use the library. The library is open to the Budapest and Hungarian academic community without restrictions, and it counts numerous patrons from the outside the university. Students, academics and professionals from all other Budapest universities, from research institutes and from many private and public organizations, including the government, use the

CEU's library and its unique resources. In many disciplines, students from outside the CEU could not write their theses without these resources. When, as planned, the CEU moves to Vienna in 2019-2020, the library will be the most significant loss for the Budapest academic community. That is an important reason why so many of them have protested openly against their government and in support of the CEU. The CEU library is a gem, architecturally and intellectually, and also a place of work, reflection and interaction, currently helping to hold together, to anchor the Budapest academic community.

National

Democracy and the right to education
The CEU is not the only academic institution in Hungary that has come under ferocious attack by the current Hungarian government (Matei and Orosz 2017; Ignatieff and Roch 2018). All research institutes of the Hungarian Academy of Sciences, the temple of science in Hungary for almost 200 years, are facing the threat of closure. Gender studies at the master's level were banned by a government decree in 2018. The Hungarian Constitution was modified in 2010 and the principles of academic freedom and institutional autonomy were abolished. The Higher Education Law was modified in 2017 through a procedure that was characterized as dictatorial[4]. Local institutions, universities included, have very little leverage to oppose such measures, even to simply protest publicly. The CEU became the catalyst of a large movement in favour of democracy and the right to education, involving not only higher education institutions and professionals, but also ordinary citizens. A series of demonstrations under the banner "free country – independent university" took place in 2017-2018, some of them bringing together close to 100,000 people on a single day. While the CEU did not organize any of these demonstrations, its

---

[4] Many Hungarian universities, the Hungarian Academy of Sciences, and the Hungarian Rectors Conference denounced publicly the illegal nature of the procedure by which the law was adopted and some also protested against its dictatorial nature. For an analysis of the overall nature of the Hungarian political regime, see, for example, Patrick Kingsley's article" On the surface, Hungary Is a Democracy. But What Lies Underneath?" in the New York Time, December 25, 2018, available at https://www.nytimes.com/2018/12/25/world/europe/hungary-democracy-orban.html, accessed February 28, 2019.

actions, including public statements, contributed to identifying and shedding light on a significant problem in Hungarian society: the anti-democratic backlash of the current government, affecting not only education but the country's entire social and political life. The European Commission has started legal proceedings against Hungary, alleging the infringement of European legislation on academic freedom and the right of establishment in the case of "Lex CEU".

Regional

Roma education

The CEU has the only programme in the world preparing young Roma for admission to graduate schools (as well as other programmes for Roma). The rationale for starting this programme was to help Roma from the CEE region to acquire the necessary competence to compete successfully for a place in master's and doctoral programmes at any university in Europe in the social sciences and related disciplines (such as public policy). The CEU believed that a graduate degree, in turn, was a necessary "entry ticket" for these Roma students to be accepted and be able to participate in public debates on behalf of their communities, as lawyers, sociologists, politicians, journalists, community activists or policy makers. In our time – the CEU reasoned – it is not possible to have access to the public arena in Europe without a master's degree, at least. Through this programme, over some 15 years, the CEU has contributed to creating an engaged Roma intelligentsia, which is not only locally - but also regionally - and European-minded. The CEU has trained a large part of the Roma intelligentsia currently active in Europe. It has acted as an anchor institution for a large, transnational/regional community and helped identify and address one of its major challenges: lack of access to the public (policy) arena due to lack of graduate qualifications among its members.

International

Academic freedom

The CEU has become a *cause célèbre* for academic freedom not only in Hungary but also in Europe and internationally. The CEU case has put the institution in a situation where its particular story helped reveal dangerous trends and limitations to academic freedom affecting students, academic and administrative staff in Europe more generally. In this way, the CEU has been able to help stimulate a European-wide reflection and action in defence of academic freedom. Many stakeholders across Europe and beyond have started engaging in actions of defence of academic freedom, alerted to or motivated by the CEU case. Once again, the CEU was able to help formulate and put on the public agenda an issue that is relevant to a specific community: the European academic community as a whole. One of the precise actions in this area was the establishment of a pan-European observatory on academic freedom in Paris, at the initiative of the CEU and foreseen to be completed in 2019-2020.

Global

Global civic society
One of the CEU's most daring projects in the recent years was the creation of a new type of School of Public Policy. The mission of this CEU School, related to the overall mission of the University, is to serve the "global civic society", rather than national governments, as most other public policy schools do. It is of course not easy or straightforward to define what the global civic society means in general or in this particular context. Some might say there is no such thing. This is a very difficult, even risky endeavour and it remains to be seen if this project will be successful. For now, it serves to illustrate the attempt to be an anchor institution at the global level: the CEU considers that one can meaningfully talk about a community of civil society stakeholders at the global level and that it can produce knowledge and train specialists to serve this community. For this, as part of its public policy degree programs and outreach activities, the CEU has developed and put in place an innovative pedagogic and professional approach that brings together students, scholars and practitioners, representatives of non-governmental and international organisations and of public authorities from around the world.

Conclusions and lessons from the particular experience of an international university: refining the concept of anchor institution

The experience of Central European University shows that higher education institutions designed to be international universities can act effectively as anchor institutions.

When serious and successful, the attempts of international universities to work as anchor institutions result in concrete benefits for identifiable communities, whether at the local, national, regional, international or even global level.

These communities, in turn, appreciate the contributions and collaboration of international universities, even when there are clear differences, for example in terms of the language of instruction in the institution vs the language spoken in the host community, the nationalities or ethnic background of the university community vs those its surrounding communities. Physical distance also does not prevent communities from supporting international universities.

Moreover, identifiable communities, from nearby or faraway, may come to the defence of international universities, which are perceived as being anchor institutions, when they face difficulties, even open attacks from external powerful forces.

The example of the CEU shows that a good test for recognizing an anchor institution is whether that institution is capable of and systematically engaged in identifying, formulating, putting on the public agenda, and effectively addressing concrete challenges and problems of clearly identifiable communities, whether at the local, national, regional, international, or global level.

References

Ehlenz, M. M. (2018): "Defining University Anchor Institution Strategies: Comparing Theory to Practice." Planning Theory & Practice 19 (1): 74-92

Fotakis, C., Rosenmöller, M., Brennan, J., Matei, L., Nikolov, R., Petiot, C., and Puukka, J. (2014): The role of Universities and Research Organisations as drivers for Smart Specialisation at regional level. Brussels EU Directorate-General for Research and Innovation, available at http://ec.europa.eu/research/regions/pdf/publications/ExpertReport-Universities_and_Smart_Spec-WebPublication-A4.pdf, accessed February 25, 2019

Goodman, E. P. (2014): "Smart Cities" Meet 'Anchor Institutions': The Case for Broadband and the Public Library." Fordham Urban Law Journal 41 (5): 1665-1694

Ignatieff, M. and Roch, S. (2018): *Academic freedom: the global challenge*. Budapest: CEU Press

Matei, L. (2008): "International by design: Institutional Strategies and Policies of an International University in Central Europe." In Gaebel, M. (ed). *Internationalisation of European higher education: an EUA/ACA handbook*. Berlin: Raabe Academic Publishers

Matei, L. and Orosz. K. (2017): "Central European University: An Exceptional Moment for Hungary, and for International Higher Education." World Education News + Reviews, June 6, 2017. Available at https://wenr.wes.org/2017/06/central-european-university-an-exceptional-moment-for-hungary-and-higher-educations-international-ambitions, accessed February 25, 2019

Maurrasse, D. J. (2002): "High Education-Community Partnerships: Assessing Progress in the Field." Nonprofit & Voluntary Sector 31(1): 131-139

Maurrasse, D (this volume): "What is an Anchor Institution and Why?"

Smallbone, D., Kitching, J., Blackburn, R. and Mosavi, S. (2015): Anchor institutions and small firms in the UK: A review of the literature on anchor institutions and their role in developing management and leadership skills in small firms. UK Commission for Employment and Skills

Smith, J.H. (2018): "Universities and their communities – Role of anchor institutions: European policy perspectives.". In Bergan, S and Harkavy, I. (eds) *Higher Education for Diversity, social inclusion and community: a democratic imperative*. Strasbourg: Council of Europe Publishing Council of Europe Higher Education Series No. 22, pp. 193-199

CHAPTER 10
THE THIRD MISSION OF UNIVERSITIES – EXAMPLES
OF "GOOD PRACTICE" (CZECH REPUBLIC)

Radka Wildova, Tomáš Fliegl, and Barbora Vokšická

Introduction

At the turn of the previous and the present millennia, the role of universities and other higher education institutions abroad, and later even in our country, has gradually begun to change considerably. In addition to the emphasis on quality education and highly specialized scientific and research efforts, the transfer of knowledge developed at higher education institutions has become increasingly relevant, useful for further research, but also for industry and the broader social development. This process is generally called the "third mission" of higher education institutions and becomes, alongside education and research, an equally important pillar of the mission and further development of universities.

The local mission of higher education institutions

The "third mission" of higher education institutions – service to broader society – leads, among other things, to the transfer of knowledge to industry, the results of which are products of applied scientific research (e.g. pharmaceuticals, nanotechnology products, etc.). However, the cooperation of higher education institutions with local organizations, with city councils and municipalities, or institutions with regional or national activities (projects of cooperation with civic associations, social services, cultural institutions, etc.) is equally important.

While the development of the "third mission" of higher education institutions may give the impression that universities are replacing or substituting for often poorly functioning public services, it is in fact a close collaboration with the application of knowledge and experience of the highest quality. Similarly, it is also the case with the above-mentioned transfer of knowledge into manufacturing practice. The public has a reason to demand that what is being tested and empirically verified should be used in everyday life.

In the following section, we present some examples of good practice from the Czech Republic that can act not only as inspiration but also as evidence that collaboration between higher education institutions and local (regional) entities is both beneficial and desirable.

UniON - Civil university

Project *"UniON - Civil university"* (Občanská univerzita) led by Palacký University in Olomouc brings together academic staff and students who voluntarily visit local communities throughout the region organizing lectures, organizing debates on a wide range of topics, meeting with local residents and sharing knowledge with them. There are several priority topics, which include legal and financial literacy, debt counselling, critical information evaluation, history, medical prevention or information for helping to manage crises (UniON – Civil University). The project focuses on the socially disadvantaged regions of the country and offers free legal services, health assistance and lifelong learning courses. Main topics discussed in these lifelong learning courses are Europe, the European Union, the state of the world or the causes of migration. Volunteers want to show that science and research are one important way of ensuring a decent future. Civil University is a platform based on a partnership approach and mutual dialogue with the public (Jasanská 2018). The concept and know-how is provided to other institutions that are interested in similar activities. The aim of the project is to maximize the opening of the academic sphere and its capacities, which will lead to mutual interaction and enrichment (Franta 2018). One of the first workshops in April 2018 took place in orphanages, where volunteers educated children about personal finances and family budgets (UniON – Civil University 2018). During the first year of operation, the project carried out six workshops on financial literacy – the basics of money management and consumer credit, Public service media: television, radio, ČTK (Czech Press Office), Civilization diseases, Antibiotics, Physics – Optics and Media representation of minorities.

"Stužák" – Students for pupils

This project connects students from all over the Czech Republic. Its name Stužák is a blend of the Czech "Students for pupils". Stužák is a platform of student associations and several other organizations. University students voluntarily organize interactive workshops and games for high school students. The aim of the project is to enhance civic education of young people – the creators strive for an active and critically-minded society. Stužák currently holds eleven different types of workshops in six basic categories: political science, international law, critical thinking, law, sociology and economics. All topics are taught using interactive and playful methods. Volunteers try to break the frontal style of instructions and take advantage of various forms of simulations, such as court hearings or role-playing. Stužák is currently formed by several student associations from universities across the Czech Republic, as well as by organizations supporting education. Student associations involved in the platform are: Agora (Faculty of Education, Charles University), the Club of Young Political scientist (Faculty of International Relations, University of Economics in Prague), Miroslava and the Political Science Club (Faculty of Social Sciences, Charles University) and the Political Science Club (Palacký University in Olomouc). Other organizations and entities involved in project are the Institute for Economic Education, the Centre for Behavioural Experiments and project Názorování (project that aims to improve debating skills) (Stužák). The novelty product of the platform is the educational board game called *"To letí století"* (It's a Century), made for the anniversary of the Czech state, about Czech history. To deliver the project, students had to create a crowd-funding campaign to raise money (HITHIT).

Projekt Symbios
An interesting example of cooperation between the university and the public sector is the project Symbios, aiming at creating a common space for people leaving the children's homes, and students of the Masaryk University (Symbios). The project is based on the cooperation between the Masaryk University, the city of Brno and non-governmental organizations. Social workers from Brno (who work with young adults), municipality and the Masaryk University have been key partners from the beginning (Masaryk University 2018). This unique project combines two groups of young people who do not usually meet in real life. Young adults leaving orphanages have complicated lives, especially during their first time of independence after leaving the home (MU Annual report 2016:62). In order to make this transition easier, they will live on slightly lower rents. Students of Masaryk University who are involved in the project come from the Faculty of Social Studies, the Faculty of Education and the Faculty of Economics and Administration. For them, it is a unique opportunity and a

possibility to gain experience related to their studies. During the autumn semester of 2018, project representatives selected prospective tenants. Participants first met during a weekend get-together, which was designed for them to get acquainted. The first tenants should start moving in at the beginning of 2019 (Fojtů 2018b).

Fakescape

The Fakescape project was devised by six students from the Institute of Political Science of Masaryk University. Students, at their own initiative, focus on the current, ever-increasing, problem of fake news and link it to an escape game, which is a modern trend. Students created the escape game in order to combat misinformation. The Fakescape game is intended for secondary school students. University students came up with the idea in autumn 2018 and now they are running its pilot phase (Fojtů 2018a). The game is designed for a group of twenty to thirty students and lasts 45 minutes (one school lesson). The aim of the game is to gather the evidence and find a way out of the locked room. Fakescape consists of four tasks in which players are involved in verifying information, working with text, exploring news headlines and photo manipulation. Everything is set within a context of a story where the main character is a journalist working during the period before the presidential election in 2028. The last part of the game is dedicated to a discussion to reflect on the activity. Students will experience the role of journalists who play an important part in distinguishing between truth and manipulation, and facts and misinformation. They will have to face manipulative techniques, scrutinize information, search for quality resources and work together as a team. The aim is to help children recognize manipulations and fake news and deepen their media literacy (Fakescape).

Agro-forestry: a chance for regional development and the sustainability of rural landscapes

The Faculty of Tropical Agriculture of the Czech University of Life Sciences Prague is implementing a project called "Agro-forestry - a chance for regional development and the sustainability of rural landscapes" in cooperation with the Central Bohemian and South Moravian Region (Czech University of Life Science Prague Annual Report 2017). The aim of the project is to evaluate the benefits, possibilities and barriers of the application of agro-forestry systems in the Czech Republic with a primary focus on the socio-economic, legislative and environmental context. This is done by the assessment of tree planting in arable land in the areas affected by soil erosion and drought and animal breeding. Expected outcome of project is certified methodology of "Implementation of agro-forestry systems on agricultural land in terms of legislative, natural and economic conditions of the Czech Republic" and workshops for farmers to raise farmers' awareness and knowledge of agro-forestry. The first workshop dedicated to educating communities took place in December 2018. The event was intended for professionals, target users (farmers, municipalities, and agricultural enterprises), research and academic staff, students, state administration and administration staff and representatives of the Central Bohemian and South Moravian Regions (Chládová 2018).

Noc venku – A Night Outdoors
A Night Outdoors is a unique event, which dates back to 2012. One of the main organizers is the Institute of Social Work of the University of Hradec Králové. The project aim is to help homeless people, to inform society about their problems and show up what does their life look like. During the event visitors could stay outdoors through whole night and experience homeless life. The event begins in the evening with concerts and theatre performances. Throughout the event a collection of winter clothing, footwear, blankets and sleeping bags for charity takes place. At night time, the programme moves to the Church of the Lord's Heart, where two films made by students are screened. Films were followed by discussions with homeless people. They talk about their day-to-day concerns, health status, quality of life, and chances for a better life. The highlight of the event is that some of the bravest participants do not return to their homes, but they try to find out what it is like to sleep outside during a winter night instead (Střítecká 2018). The creators of the project want to point out the risks of homelessness, reduce the prejudice against the homeless, familiarize the public with the lives of homeless people and families to draw attention to the ever-increasing number of people without long-term, high quality housing. The goal is to educate through experience. They seek to improve the status and capabilities of homeless people in society and to change public attitudes towards homelessness. They open up space to discuss the

problem of homelessness in a comprehensive way and to express its solidarity in various ways.

Faculty of Medicine, Masaryk University

Medical students of the Faculty of Medicine of Masaryk University take an active role in various awareness raising campaigns aimed at the general public. For example, they hold a traditional World Day of Diabetes Awareness event. The event is organized annually by the international non-profit organization IFMSA and involves the cooperation of all eight faculties of medicine all over the Czech Republic (Wiesnerová 2018). The aim of one of the latest events held in November 2018 was to raise awareness about diabetes prevention. At the event, people could have their blood sugar (glycemia) levels, blood pressure, and the percentage of body fat measured. In addition, they could practice first aid and self-examination for cancer. There were also dentistry students who presented the correct method of teeth cleaning, and a teddy bear hospital for children (Masaryk University 2018).

Street Law - Experience the Law Differently

The project Street Law - Experience the Law Differently, has been operating within the Faculty of Law of Charles University continuously since 2009, making it the longest-running Street Law project in the Czech Republic. The aim of the Street Law project is to help increase the legal literacy of people who do not have legal education. It was created in 1972 at Georgetown University in Washington, DC, from where it spread all over the world (Street law PF UK). In the Czech Republic, the essence of the programme is in the cooperation between law faculty and schools, public institutions or the non-profit sector. The project includes a team of teachers, students and graduates of the Faculty of Law. More than 5,300 people have been involved in it since its inception. Among the participants were students of the Faculty of Law, secondary school students, several hundred senior citizens, members of disadvantaged minorities and many others. The project started in cooperation with secondary schools only, but now the Faculty of Law cooperates for example with a group of young Romani musicians, called 'Čhavorenge', the Pankrác Prison, or senior citizens (Charles University Annual Report 2017: 25). More advanced students prepare interactive lessons for school pupils under the pedagogical supervision of faculty members. The project is not limited to legal knowledge; emphasis is also put on skills and attitudes (values that are protected by law) and especially on the use of law in practice. The university opens up to the general public and students, with the help of teachers, contribute to increasing legal literacy within society. Street Law is interactive – the goal is to attract pupils and students into the world of law, show them how law affects them, which is also reflected in the teaching methods. Project creators try to work with modern and interactive methods such as discussing specific court decisions, playing and analyze scenes with legal issues, or role-playing simulated court hearings, as this project should not only educate, but also entertain all involved (Street law PF UK).

MjUNI

MjUNI is a children's university project of the Masaryk University. MjUNI is an opportunity for children and adolescents, aged 9-17, to experience what it is like to be a university student. Students will become acquainted with the academic environment through interactive playful activities and will visit top research institutes, where they will expand their knowledge of humanities, natural sciences and technical sciences. Thanks to the interactive program, children gain new experience and skills that they can apply in future studies (MjUNI). MjUNI aims to popularize science among young students, their families and the general public by using interesting and innovative ways of teaching, the university tries to inspire children and adolescents to learn outside of school classrooms and deepen their relationship with learning (Masaryk University Annual Report 2017: 95). Thematically structured blocks of teaching represent the Masaryk University as a diverse and welcoming environment, taking care of education and development. Schooling takes place at all 9 faculties. Children's academic year starts in October and ends in July. Lectures and workshops are held during the academic year on one Saturday each month. After successful completion of the course, each student obtains a diploma with the signature of the Chancellor at the graduation ceremony (MjUNI).

Junior university

Junior university is a project of Charles University, the oldest university in the Czech Republic. The programme is designed for secondary school students from across the country. Junior university, which has been taking place for the fourth year, is an interesting way to introduce university education and environment to secondary school students (Junior Charles University). The programme aims are to popularize science and research, to raise awareness of the university, to bring students closer to the university environment and, last but not least, to increase the interest of potential applicants in university studies. The students can attend various lectures organized by faculties in collaboration with other experts. The lectures have two main areas of interest: science (medicine) and humanities. In 2017, 220 high school students took part in the project and 14 Charles University Faculties were involved (Charles University Annual Report 2017: 21).

Senior Citizens' Education

Most higher education institutions also focus on supporting senior citizens' education through their so-called Senior Citizens' Universities or Universities of the Third Age. The aim of this is to allow senior citizens to study certain disciplines at a university for a year, outside of regular study programmes, receiving a certificate upon successful completion. For the senior citizens, this is not only an opportunity to gain new insights, but also to meet with peers over common interests, to be members of the academic environment, and finally, to spend their leisure time meaningfully. Courses for senior citizens are very popular, especially topics such as "Music Topography", "the Philosophy of Education" and "Popular Chemical Experiments".

Conclusion

Higher education institutions in the Czech Republic are developing their so-called "third mission" in addition to education, science and research, the purpose of which is, above all, to transfer knowledge and experience into the everyday lives of citizens. This role is relatively new for Czech higher education institutions and therefore every university is looking for the best way to support and further develop it.

One of the results of this endeavour was, for example, the creation of the Centre for Knowledge and Technology Transfer at the Charles University and, later, the creation of a subsidary company that is wholly owned by the Charles University - Charles University Innovations Prague (CUIP). First results have already emerged – CUIP has recently entered into a large-scale contract with a renowned US pharmaceutical company to sell research findings in the field of tuberculosis treatment.

It is not only the economy that benefits from the third mission of universities. Though it may appear that the main flow of the knowledge transfer is focused just on natural sciences as well as on biomedicine, it is necessary to emphasize the growing importance of the cooperation between public administration on the one hand and the humanities on the other. This is one of the most promising areas of cooperation, and one that was not foreseen before the launching of the "third mission movement".

Another important experience drawn from the third mission is the still growing self-awareness of the higher education institution in terms of their involvement in public debate on key political issues, namely the defense of civil society, freedom and democracy, and with the fight against fake news by insisting on rational arguments and proven facts being particularly important.

References

Charles University. Annual Report 2017. https://www.cuni.cz/UK-8533-version1-annrep_2017_72dpi.pdf

Chládová, A. (2018): Nový agrolesnický projekt: Agrolesnictví – šance pro regionální rozvoj a udržitelnost venkovské krajiny [The New Agro-Forestry Project: Agro-forestry – a Chance for Regional Development and the Sustainability of Rural Landscapes]. Czech Association for Agriculture http://agrolesnictvi.cz/?p=755 accessed December 14, 2018.

Czech University of Life Science Prague. Annual Report 2017. https://www.czu.cz/en/r-7210-o-czu/r-7702-oficialni-dokumenty/r-7812-vyrocni-zpravy

Fakescape. O nás [About Us]. fakescape.cz. http://fakescape.cz/nas-tym/ accessed December 14, 2018.

Fojtů, M. (2018a): Studenti bojují s dezinformacemi pomocí únikové hry Fakescape [Students Combat Misinformation with the Escape Game Fakescape]. online.muni.cz.

https://www.online.muni.cz/student/11092-studenti-bojuji-s-dezinformacemi-pomoci-unikove-hry-fakescape accessed December 14, 2018.

Fojtů, M. (2018b): Studenti pomůžou lidem odcházejícím z dětských domovů. Budou bydlet společně [Students Will Help People Leaving Orphanages. They Will Be Living Together]. online.muni.cz.

https://www.online.muni.cz/udalosti/10266-projekt-symbios-nabidne-pomoc-lidem-odchazejicim-z-detskych-domovu accessed December 14, 2018.

Franta, T. (2018): UP představuje Občanskou univerzitu. S projektem UniON vyrazí do regionu [UP Introduces the Civil University. UniON Goes to the Region with the Project UniOn]. Žurnál online zpravodajství z Univerzity.

https://www.zurnal.upol.cz/nc/pl/zprava/clanek/up-predstavuje-obcanskou-univerzitu-s-projektem-union-vyrazi-do-regionu/, accessed on January 12, 2019.

HITHIT. Stužák - interaktivní workshopy pro středoškoláky [Stužák – Interactive Workshops for High School Students]. hithit.com. https://www.hithit.com/cs/project/5409/stuzak-interaktivni-workshopy-pro-stredoskolaky accessed December 14, 2018.

Jasanská, M. (2018) Univerzita odstartovala projekt UniON [The University Started the Project UniON]. union.upol.cz http://union.upol.cz /zprava/clanek/univerzita-odstartovala-projekt-union/ accessed December 14, 2018.

Junior Charles University. Juniorská univerzita Karlova [Junior Charles University]. juniorskauniverzita.cuni.cz https://www.juniorskauniverzita.cuni.cz/JU-88.html accessed December 14, 2018.

Masaryk University (2018): Projekt Symbios nabídne pomoc lidem odcházejícím z dětských domovů [The Project Symbios Offers Help to People Leaving Orphanages]. Muni.cz https://www.muni.cz/pro-media/tiskove-zpravy/projekt-symbios-nabidne-pomoc-lidem-odchazejicim-z-detskych-domovu accessed December 14, 2018.

Masaryk University. Annual Report 2016.

https://www.muni.cz/o-univerzite/uredni-deska/vyrocni-zpravy-mu-a-soucasti, accessed January 12, 2019.

Masaryk University. Annual Report 2017.

https://www.muni.cz/o-univerzite/uredni-deska/vyrocni-zpravy-mu-a-soucasti, accessed January 12, 2019.

Masaryk University (2018): Medici vám změří riziko diabetu. Stánky otevřou v Olympii [Medicine Students Will Measure Your Risk of Diabetes. They Will Have Stands in Olympia]. online.muni.cz.

https://www.online.muni.cz/student/11104-medici-vam-zmeri-riziko-diabetua accessed December 14, 2018.

MjUNI. O nás [About Us]. mjuni.cz https://mjuni.cz/o-nas accessed December 14, 2018.

Street law PF UK. Street law na Pf UK. streetlaw.eu http://streetlaw.eu/street-law-na-pf-uk/ accessed December 14, 2018.

Střítecká, V. (2018): První hradecká Noc venku si našla své fanoušky [The First Hradec Night Outdoors Found Its Fans]. uhk.cz

https://www.uhk.cz/cs-CZ/USP/Novinky/Prvni-hradecka-Noc-venku-si-nasla-sve-fanousky accessed December 14, 2018.

Stužák. Stužák-Spolky [Stužák-Clubs]. stužák.cz. https://stuzak.cz/spolky accessed December 14, 2018

Stužák. Stužák-Workshopy [Stužák-Workshops]. stužák.cz. https://stuzak.cz/objednavka/workshopy accessed December 14, 2018

Symbios. O nás [About Us]. symbiosbrno.cz https://www.symbiosbrno.cz/ accessed December 14, 2018

UniON – Civil University. (2018): Projekt UniON – Občanská univerzita má za sebou první výjezdy [The Project UniON – Civil University Made its First Trips]. union.upol.cz https://union.upol.cz/zprava/clanek/projekt-union-obcanska-univerzita-ma-za-sebou-prvni-vyjezdy/ accessed January 12, 2019.

UniON – Civil University. O projektu – Základní informace [About the Project – Basic Information]. Union.upol.cz https://union.upol.cz/o-projektu/ accessed December 14, 2019.

Wiesnerová, E. (2018): Medici v akci: Studenti vysvětlovali, jak pečovat o zdraví [Medicine Students in Action: Students Were Explaining How to Take Care of Your Health]. online.muni.cz.

https://www.online.muni.cz/student/10646-medici-v-akci-studenti-vysvetlovali-jak-pecovat-o-zdravia accessed December 14, 2018.

BROADER PERSPECTIVES

CHAPTER 11
THE LOCAL MISSION OF HIGHER EDUCATION: A GLOBAL VIEW

Pam Fredman

The traditional and current view of the role of universities and other higher education institutions is to create, develop and disseminate knowledge through research, teaching and learning. Knowledge knows no geographical boundary; it is designed to be disseminated and shared worldwide.

The United Nations (UN) highlights the key role of higher education institutions for Agenda 2030[1] (United Nations 2015). In April 2017, Peter Thomson (Thomson 2017), at the time President of the United Nations General Assembly, sent out a letter to all leaders of higher education institutions around the world, using the IAU World Higher Education Database[2] and saying *"It goes without saying that young people are the most capable of the transformation required, having the most to gain or lose, from the success or failure, of the Agenda 2030. I therefore make this sincere request to you to make these goals an integral part of research, teaching and study at your institutions."*

The global responsibility does not exclude local activities. On the contrary, the local mission of higher education in society is part of the role of higher education in the development of sustainable societies. The success of knowledge formation and knowledge transfer through higher education depends on its being appreciated and supported by political leaders and all sectors of society.

Therefore, it is crucial that the universities reach out through their teachers and students and become part of community development at the local level. The public and private institutions must actively participate in local cooperation in order for the community to benefit from new knowledge and competence. It is also crucial for the community to contribute to defining relevant research issues and to

---

[1] Agenda 2030 is a framework for actions needed for a sustainable development adopted by UN General Assembly 2015 in resolution A/RES/70/1 with the title "Transforming our world - the Agenda 2030 for sustainable development". The documents comprise 17 sustainable development goals (SDGs), which have been adopted by193 countries.

[2] www.whed.net, accessed January 8, 2019

help identify future needs for competence. In recent years, the local involvement and responsibility of higher education has gained increased attention at international conferences where higher education institutions and organizations linked to higher education present many initiatives and not only discuss their successes, but also identify some obstacles to success of a global nature. A reflection from these meetings is that many of the common global concerns coupled to the social mission of higher education go beyond the higher education sector itself and extend to politics and policy, to the broader private and public sectors and civil society, but they are rarely or never represented at those meetings.

It is important to understand that cooperation between higher education and other actors must build on trust in and respect for each other's roles and goals. Higher education has a unique role to play in knowledge creation through research, teaching, and learning based on principles and core values that are a hallmark of higher education and to which higher education institutions around the world commit through the Magna Charta Universitatum (MCU)[3]. These values are shared by members of the International Association of Universities (IAU)[4] and other higher education organizations and networks. To freely undertake research and disseminate knowledge are fundamental values of higher education. The core values also comprise institutional autonomy as well as social responsibility locally and globally. Last but not least, the competences our students acquire through higher education should include deep understanding of the disciplines in which they specialize as well as advanced transversal competences valid regardless of academic discipline. The students are the future leaders and decision makers in politics, business, the public sector, civil society etc. and they need to be trained in critical thinking and develop their analytical capacity to guide society towards sustainable development.

While the role of higher education in society could be seen as global there is wide-spread diversity in national and local criteria for academic performance and approaches to developing cooperation between higher education and local stakeholders. National diversity comprises, the balance between public and non-public funding of

---

[3] http://www.magna-charta.org/index.html, accessed January 8, 2019.
[4] https://www.iau-aiu.net/, accessed January 8, 2019

higher education and support and promotion of local cooperation between higher education and other stakeholders. There is also diversity in national contexts - e.g. in laws and regulations, that might be an issue when applying successful examples of local projects from other countries. One concern is also if the fundamental values, described above, are universal. Local diversity is extensive and comprises not only local needs and challenges but also socioeconomic conditions, primary and secondary education quality and access, private and public labour markets, geographic and climate conditions etc.

Thus, there is no universal model for cooperation between higher education and broader society. For the same reason, it is difficult to identify national or international common criteria for measuring and comparing the success of each type of cooperation. Evaluation of social impact, or social engagement, is becoming part of research and higher education as exemplified by the REF in England and NISA in Australia[5]. However, the exercise has proven difficult. In a recent publication from TEFCE (TEFCE 2018) the needs of moving away from quantitative indicators to qualitative assessment procedures for evaluating the broader perspective of social impact and engagement is highlighted. In Sweden, a new quality assessment system for institutional performance in education and research is now in operation, and social impact is evaluated as part of this exercise[6]. The social impact coupled to education and research is to be described by the institution in its self-evaluation report.

One global concern that was raised at a recent IAU event (IAU 2018) was that the very fact that there are no widely agreed measurable indicators also means that success cannot be reflected properly in today's ranking systems, thus reducing the interest in the local mission of higher education institutions. The lack of holistic views and adaption to the changes in the role of higher education in current national and

---

[5] Impact and engagement asssement is found in The English Research Excellence Framework REF, https://www.ref.ac.uk/ and a similar in the Australian NISA, National Innovation Science agenda, https://www.arc.gov.au/engagement-and-impact-assessment, both accessed February 14, 2019.

[6] http://english.uka.se/quality-assurance/quality-assurance-of-higher-education.html, accessed January 8, 2019

international ranking systems opens the question about the strong impact of ranking. University World News (Seneviratne, 2018) reported a speech given by the Minister of Education in Singapore, Ong Ye Kung, in which he questioned "international ranking systems' ability to take into account the varied and profound roles of universities today". Moreover, the article also mentioned that the Singapore International Academic Advisory Panel, consisting of higher education leaders and CEOs of global companies, has recommended that Singapore develop a holistic evaluation framework for research and higher education.

The local mission of higher education is multifaceted, and a global concern raised at the IAU International conference (IAU 2018) was the difficulties encountered in finding resources for local projects. This is due to the multidisciplinary character of such projects and the lack of interest from national and in particular international funders to support local initiatives. Moreover, these projects need time to develop, while funding is often based on short-sighted/short term considerations.

Local cooperation between higher education and stakeholders is likely to facilitate and speed up transfer of knowledge from higher education into practice. It will also stimulate research projects and higher education programmes with a focus on local needs and challenges. Increasing translation and dissemination of new knowledge at the local level through the work of faculty and students will contribute to the public and private sector and civil society. However, to provide incentives for faculty and students to engage in local missions this must be given weight in ensuring employment and furthering academic advancement both inside and outside the higher education

Campus presence is today not necessary for providing access to higher education in the local community. New technology, including digitalization, provides excellent opportunities for distance teaching and learning. However, one concern is that the physical distance between the local community and the institution may reduce the attractiveness for faculty to be involved in projects with local stakeholders, especially as such participation is felt to take time away from doing basic research. In a context in which competition for academic services and research funding is fierce, publications numbers - preferably in highly ranked journals - is what counts most for academic advancement today. There is a global responsibility of higher education systems but also research funders and other stakeholders to recognize and value the local mission of higher education in terms of academic prestige, funding, and advancement.

The importance and relevance of local presence of higher education for community development for providing competence to the local public and business sector and for the economic growth has been reported[7]. In Sweden, a large country with a low population density outside of the large cities, this perspective is crucial for meeting the local need for school teachers and staff of social institutions and health care and local business. From my own experience from Gothenburg, the presence of higher education in the city meant a lot for the identification and definition of the societal competence needs, including for the large international industries in the area and the establishment of new companies. One example is the development of the car industry, where there is a long tradition of close cooperation between the local higher education institutions and the industry both in the exchange of staff and the possibility of students to gain practical experience. This has built a unique competence in all areas involving industrial development and production.

Another example is the mining and steel industry in the north of Sweden, which depends on the local higher education institutions to recruit labour, since there is noticeable resistance among most graduates from elsewhere to move to that part of Sweden. These are examples from Sweden but there are likely similar examples in many other countries. Thus, both access to higher education and development of competences locally are important factors for the business sector and are certainly important for attracting new businesses.

One role of higher education is to create and disseminate knowledge responding to global responsibility for the UN sustainable development goals[8] and the local mission must include this perspective. Local cooperation in most cases brings stakeholders closer and make mutual benefits easier to acknowledge, which does not exclude social impact globally. I will give an example from my experience as Rector at the University of Gothenburg. The city's two

---

[7] Articles on this topic have been published for some years with a focus on economic development. Examples are a German study (Winterhagen and Krücken,2015, Spain, Europe and North America (Aranguran *et al.*, 2016) and a study of industrial PhD schools (Gustavsson *et al.* 2016)

[8] https://sustainabledevelopment.un.org/?menu=1300, accessed January 8, 2019.

universities, the bus industry and the Gothenburg municipality together started and still run local projects on electric and self-driving buses. Teachers/researchers and students at the master and doctoral level from various disciplines and experts from the industry and from the municipality work together. The city is the living laboratory and the project is favoured by the local presence of all actors, but the results are of interest for the global market.

Rapid technological developments and their introduction in society place demands on access to competence, and this applies to the technical and medical as well as social sciences and humanities. Higher education must rise to these challenges, which include the opportunity for today's labour force to upgrade its competences through Lifelong Learning (Bologna Process 2001). This is a mission of higher education, and the local availability of higher education is a requirement. Lifelong Learning does put huge demands on higher education institutions and will require that they cooperate with employers to define the specific needs for competence and the possibility that their employees take part in Lifelong Learning courses. This category of prospective students is less likely to move to study somewhere else; it will rather look to access local higher education opportunities.

Not least, cooperation between higher education and society, the private and public sectors, and civil society through staff exchange is a valuable tool in the local mission of higher education. Academic staff will not only transfer knowledge but also get practical perspectives and demands on knowledge development, which might increase the social impact of research and higher education. The students will gain practical perspectives when staff and expert practitioners from outside higher education participate in lectures. Such staff exchange will almost only be possible in a local context. In this context it is necessary to underline that funding of higher education to increase access and success will require support from politicians, who need to recognize higher education as a public good (Bologna Process 2003).

The local mission of HE is multifaceted and involves stakeholders from all parts of society and for successful development there are concerns that all stakeholders need to respond to.
These include:

- The unique role of higher education institutions, including the principles and core values they uphold, must be publicly defended by political decision makers and be respected by society for trustful cooperation with mutual benefits;

- The merit of experience from local cooperation must be valued and recognized by the higher education sector, research funding agencies and employers in society;
- Experience from practice in society as part of higher education programmes must be recognized and rewarded with credits and recognized by employers;
- Assessment tools, with a holistic approach, for the evaluation of local social impact must be developed at the national and international levels and reflected in rankings;
- Funding agencies, national and international, must be more open to high quality multidisciplinary projects and recognize the value of local cooperation projects and their potential future global impact.

To stimulate further work at national, European and international levels, politicians, higher education leadership, funding agencies and organizations, private and public employers, and civil society all need to reduce the obstacles to the successful development of higher education locally. A common voice for the recognition of the relevance of the local mission of higher education is needed.

References

Anguran, M.J., et al. (2016): Academic institutions as change agents for territorial development, Industry and Higher education, vol 30, no1, pp 27-40

Bologna Process (2001): "Towards the European Higher Education Area". Communiqué of the meeting of European Ministers in charge of Higher Education in Prague on May 19th 2001, available at http://www.ehea.info/ media.ehea.info/file/2001_Prague/44/2/2001_Prague_Communique_English_55 3442.pdf, accessed January 22, 2019

Bologna Process (2003): "Realising the European Higher Education Area", Communiqué of the Conference of Ministers responsible for Higher Education in Berlin on 19 September 2003, available at http://www.ehea.info/ media.ehea.info/file/2003_Berlin/28/4/2003_Berlin_Communique_English_5772 84.pdf, accessed January 22, 2019

Gustavsson L.;Call N. and Söderlind J (2016): "An impact analysis of regional industry university interaction: the case of industrial PhD schools", Industry and higher education, vol 30, no 1, pp41-51

IAU (2018): "Higher education partnership for social impact" International Conference 2018, available at https://www.eiseverywhere.com/ehome /index.php?eventid=251326&, accessed January 8, 2019

NISA, National Innovation Science agenda, https://www.arc.gov.au/ engagement-and-impact-assessment, accessed February 14, 2019

REF, The English Research Excellence Framework REF, https://www.ref.ac.uk/, accessed February 14, 2019

Seneviratne K (2018): "Rethink the role of HE beyond rankings" University World News, issue 253, October 3, 2018, https://www.university worldnews.com/post.php?story=20181003174150435, accessed January 23, 2019

TEFCE (2018): TEFCE Policy Brief#1, Towards a European Framework for Community Engagement, December 2018

Thomson, Peter (2017): "To Leaders of Universities and other Higher Education Institutions around the World", 24 May 2017, http://www.iau-hesd.net/en/news/4742-letter-peter-thomson-leaders-universities-and-other-higher-education-institutions-around, accessed January 23, 2019

UKÄ Swedish Higher Education Authority, Quality Assurance of Higher Education and Research. http://english.uka.se/quality-assurance/quality-assurance-of-higher-education.html/, accessed January 22, 2019

United Nations (2015): The Sustainable Development Agenda, available at https://www.un.org/sustainabledevelopment/development-agenda/, accessed January 8, 2019

Winterhagen N. and Krücken G,(2015): "The local war for talent; recruitment of recent tertiary education graduates from a regional perspective; some evidence from a German case", European Journal of Higher Education, vol 5,no 2, pp127-140.

CHAPTER 12
ENGAGEMENT AS TRANSFORMATIVE: A SOUTH AFRICAN EXAMPLE

Ahmed Bawa

Introduction

Public and Community Engagement features in Research England's very recent Knowledge Exchange Framework consultation document as one of the perspectives for measurement which will likely be linked to research funding (Research England 2018). Browsing through the Australian open access journal *Transform*, one finds a growing consensus about the importance of engagement to universities there. This is a journal of Engagement Australia described as "a peak alliance of Australian higher education institutions focused on how education connects with communities for mutual benefit" (Transform 2018). A growing body of writing in Europe is beginning to address the need for universities to engage in more serious ways with their publics. Some of this work is supported by the Council of Europe's Education Department in its collaboration with the International Consortium for Higher Education, Civic Responsibility and Democracy. And in a similar vein South Africa's 26 public universities, speaking through Universities South Africa, have agreed to elevate engagement into a transformational project, one that addresses the transformative impact of engagement on institutional culture, the construction of new relationships with the publics of institutions and the development of synergistic knowledge-based partnerships.

Background to engagement in South Africa

South Africa's universities share a long and interesting history of engagement which influenced the drafting of the Higher Education Act of 1997 (Department of Education 1997), which in turn influenced engagement during the post-1997 period. These documents were supplemented by other policy interventions such as the specific funding of engagement-related research by the National Research Foundation (NRF). The creation of the National System of Innovation, of which the universities are the largest part, was designed to foster higher levels of social and industrial innovation and to ensure greater levels of synergy between the knowledge enterprise and the processes of social and political reconstruction and development (National Advisory Council on Innovation 2017). The promulgation of the Higher Education Act also brought into being the Council of Higher Education to create a functioning higher education quality system that would provide the necessary quality platforms for the development of ethical, high quality engagement partnerships and the evolution of institutional policy initiatives to promote engagement. (CHE 2019). And yet, it is probably true that the extent to which engagement gripped the imagination of higher education has declined since 1990.

There are two major reasons for this. While higher education policy sought to create an impetus towards increasingly higher levels of engagement, the formal funding system of universities did not recognize engagement as a funding category. Attempts by the university system to engage the government on this matter were unsuccessful. Interestingly, and correctly, the response of the state has always been that this is core university business – covered as it is in the Higher Education Act – and that therefore institutions should prioritize institutional funding, from both public and private sources, for the purpose of engagement. 'Soft funding' from foundations and donors, on which engagement activities depended, went into decline soon after 1990 and essentially came to an end in the period immediately after the democratic transition in 1994. At what was then the University of Natal, approximately 60 projects came to an end during this period (Bawa 2007). The second reason was the development of a national policy ecosystem in approximately 2005 that was designed to affect the output of research. A stagnation in research output through the late 1990s and early 2000s caused deep concern across the science system. A national data-driven policy ecosystem, involving the Department of Higher Education and Training, the Department of Science and Technology and the National Research Foundation came into effect to stimulate research output and to enhance publishing in 'global', high impact factor journals (SciSTIP 2017). Related to this, in more recent years, has been the impact of the rankings systems on those institutions that are enthusiastic participants. The national subsidy system provides the impetus for a certain level of institutional differentiation, with research intensive universities enjoying a larger share of higher education budget. Perhaps more importantly rankings have also provided for greater competitiveness for more substantial international funding opportunities. The effect of the new funding system was to stimulate institutional incentive schemes that would encourage individual academics to publish as often as possible. This drove individuals away from time-consuming engagement activities as a source of knowledge production. Under powerful funding steering mechanisms there was a rather decisive shift away from engagement as a site of knowledge production.

Notwithstanding these challenges, the tradition of academic activism and engagement that evolved during and after the years of apartheid has influenced research and development. Each university has a suite of engagement activities, though more often than not, these are driven by individuals who often face institutional impediments in their attempts to generate new institutional cultures. In their projects, the dedicated funding from the NRF has been an important impetus.

New conditions

With the recent student activism that has swept across the country, the debate and discussion about higher education engagement has received new impetus through two quite distinct paths. The first relates to student demands for a 'decolonized, quality' education. The severe instability between 2015 and 2017 due mainly to the campaign for free higher education was augmented by this much more interesting, probing demand for 'decolonized, quality' higher education which produced renewed interest on the nature of the national knowledge project evoking very substantial discussion both institutionally and nationally with a series of different thrusts emerging (Bawa 2019a). The key issue raised by students is that 24 years after the national democratic transition and the large demographic changes in the higher education system, there has not yet been a sufficient change in the knowledge project to reflect these changes; that it appears to be locked into its 'western' colonial roots. Much has been written about the various nuances of this (Leibowitz 2017). The experience of epistemic disconnection was raised repeatedly by students in their slogans.

The second relates to concerns about the chasm that appears to exist between the universities and their publics (Bawa 2019 b). This was demonstrated most effectively by the fact that when the universities were seriously under threat, in fact at the point of collapse, there was simply no defense of them from any of their natural publics. This situation raised questions about the social ownership of universities and of their role as knowledge intensive social institutions. In the context of the enormous challenges being faced by South Africa, including unacceptably high unemployment rates due to a sluggish economy, growing and deepening inequality, the deep and recurring failures in public health, the breakdown in water and waste management, this lack of legitimacy is deeply worrying.

It is probably fair to say that a new sustained discourse on engagement emerged in 2017 and 2018 much more related to the idea of the university as a social institution and has rekindled 4 interesting lines of investigation.

- The first examines the nature of academic discourse related to engagement leading to critical new understandings of the relationship between science/knowledge on the one hand and human and social development on the other, including the interrogation of competing epistemologies and pedagogies of engagement.

- The second relates to understanding what kinds of national policies would address the mainstreaming of engagement both as a sectoral and institutional activity.

- The third relates to understanding the progressive encouragement of engagement at the institutional level via the adoption of suitable policies, the construction of institutional structures and the development of strategic frameworks. Ultimately this has to do with understanding how to optimize the nature of institutions of higher learning as institutions of sustainable engagement, rather than as institutions that dip in and out of engagement.

- The fourth relates to working with the publics of the universities in developing trust, growing their capacity to be more effective in the partnerships and to begin to understand how best to measure the impact of the engagement partnerships so as to foster a culture of growth and improvement.

These lines of exploration are perceived to be the key to understanding how, in the South African context, a quadruple helix involving universities, their publics, the national higher education and science funding systems and local development agencies (such as local government departments or not-for-profit agencies) may be effectively optimized to produce results that benefit society.

Engagement as knowledge production

Notwithstanding the rich history of engagement in the South African higher education system, there has always been deep concern amongst academics that engagement took away time from what were believed to be core academic activities. Its conceptualization as the 'third' mandate of universities resulted in it being seen as an add-on to teaching/learning and research. The Council on Higher Education, through its quality audits, in its 2004 10-year review of higher education in South Africa, found that there was

> A perception that community engagement and service are merely add-on, nice-to-have, and philanthropic activities remains a key challenge to its integration as a core function in the academy.
>
> (Council on Higher Education 2007)

This has changed to some extent with the introduction of a small but dedicated programme of research funding mobilized by the National Research Foundation for high quality, peer-reviewed research based on engagement.

As pointed out earlier, recent events have reignited the need for a rigorous discourse on the role of universities as social institutions, in being more engaged in the business of shaping a society more sensitive to the agendas of social justice and human rights. This is not new rhetoric. When linked to the demands for a decolonized higher education system, the idea that teaching and research of the higher education system must develop closer and more serious connections with its publics becomes important. Needless to say, this does not mean that there ought to be an undermining of other forms of research and teaching practice but it does mean developing a higher level of responsibility to produce knowledge of the local contexts – through the design of bona fide knowledge-based development partnerships focusing both on theory and praxis. This brings to mind the very significant discussion in South Africa in the early 1990s related to Mode 2 knowledge production[1] and its relationship to engagement (Kraak 2000). How is this linked to the idea of a decolonized knowledge system? Such a system would be required to enter the global knowledge system on its own terms, one that at least assumes the responsibility for the production of knowledge of the local context, however such a context is defined. Engagement, through the formation of local knowledge-intensive partnerships, would seem to be key to such a development. This in turn would imply that we conceive of engagement as fundamental to the teaching/learning and research enterprises of institutions; as a source of knowledge production and dissemination, as contributing to the social and economic wellbeing of the various publics of institutions.

As mentioned earlier, in the run-up to the large policy exercises in the post-1994 period there was much discussion about South Africa's knowledge project, particularly to find ways to increase its articulation with the challenges of reconstruction and development. There was an interesting discussion about new modes of knowledge production shaped largely by the work of Gibbons et.al. and especially as it pertained to engagement. (Gibbons et al. 1994) That ideological moment did not permit the emergence of a more radical conceptualization of South Africa's knowledge project; and 24 years later, it took another generation of student activists to point out its inadequacies, notwithstanding the under-defined nature of that intervention.

National policies as steering mechanisms
There is excellent evidence in South Africa of how effectively national funding policy may steer institutional and system behaviour. The appearance of engagement as a third mandate of universities in the Higher Education Act of 1997 was both an important recognition of its

---

[1] The work by Gibbons, et al. (Gibbons 1994) in their pursuit of a better understanding of the ways in which the organization of knowledge production was changing as universities interacted more closely with industry was taken up by the policy discussions taking place in South Africa. What Gibbons, et al. called Mode 2 knowledge production indicated shifts towards more integrative approaches to transdisciplinary research beginning with an applications imperative rather than an academic one.

importance and an opportunity for the national state and institutions to relegate it to an unfunded mandate, resulting in cursory attention being paid to it. On the other hand, the fact that it is a specifically defined unfunded mandate resulted in a deepening dependence on donor funding for engagement activities, until donor funding became scarcer. These three factors - engagement as an unfunded mandate, the growing scarcity of donor funding and impetus to revisit the knowledge project of the public universities - probably provide the impetus for universities to consolidate an understanding of engagement as being central to their core mandates of teaching/learning and research which are the key drivers for subsidy funding to universities.

The launch by the National Research Foundation, the Department of Science and Technology's key research funding agency, of its Community Engagement Funding Instrument with the specific purpose of enhancing a better understanding by scholars 'to come to grips with some of the philosophical and conceptual challenges associated with the dynamics of community engagement and social responsiveness, as a field of research enquiry' (NRF 2016). The 'key features of the instrument' are described by the NRF as

• *Research which contributes to deeper theoretical, philosophical and conceptual orientations of community engagement from a higher education perspective;*
• *Research which interrogates the complex interplay and processes of engagement; that is, the various ways in which knowledge is produced, assimilated and utilized through interactions and relationships with communities;*

Case studies, typologies, appreciative inquiry about community engagement and community assessments. (NRF 2016: 5)

In important respects this followed some of the salient concerns raised by Lis Lange following her analysis of the institutional audits carried out by the Council of Higher Education which she expresses as *"my sense from reading the documentation that institutions produced for the audit was that this area is a very under-theorised aspect of the role of universities. An engaged university is not necessarily the same as a socially responsive university that is attuned to meeting particular skills needs. The conceptual continuum may exist on the surface, but there are more dissonances than one would imagine in the understanding of community engagement."* (Lange 2008) This, together with idea of understanding engagement as fundamentally critical to the emergence of a decolonized higher education, require us to move rapidly, to a better understanding of the place of engagement in South Africa's knowledge project. Martin Hall, in 2010, asked *"Why, then, is the imperative of community engagement regarded as radical, risqué and anything other than taken-for-granted?"* (Hall 2010: 2) notwithstanding the fact that it is contained within the Higher Education Act as a core function of universities. He suggests that the fact that *"community engagement is so regarded suggests an epistemological ambiguity in the knowledge project of our universities"* (Hall 2010: 2). This is precisely what has emerged through recent debates on the knowledge enterprise of South Africa's science system.

Institutional policies

The autonomy of South African institutions gives them control over their institutional policy development in so far as their policies are in consonance with national higher education policy. On the other hand, as mentioned above, there is very good evidence that institutional policymaking is very powerfully steered through national funding mechanisms. It is well established that the success of engagement depends fundamentally on having institutional policies that encourage, facilitate and incentivize engagement. Writing about the funding tensions between teaching/learning and research on the one hand and engagement on the other that arise at most universities, Cheryl de la Rey reflects: "Counting matters to managers of institutions in terms of the amount of funding that they receive. Therefore, we need develop a consensus perspective to bridge or address the tension, an aspect of which is how to make it measurable." (De la Rey 2008).

The important point here is the need to build consensus on the way institutional and sectoral policy engages the matter of engagement. At the first end of the spectrum are those institutions that see engagement as an add-on activity and at the second are those that have concretely integrated engagement into their core activities. Most institutions in South Africa lie somewhere on this spectrum; the further to the first end the greater the dependency on special funding, the further to the second the greater the integration of engagement into the institutional funding system. Perhaps the most important aspects of institutional policy that impact on engagement are those of academic appointments, promotions and support. And again, this depends very heavily on where on the spectrum institutions reside; which ones see engagement as viable and vital sites of teaching/learning and research.

The creation of dynamic interfaces that simultaneously face outwards and inwards to provide for the development of trusted spaces which may be both coherent and contested seems important to ensure that the universities are seen to be and to act as social institutions. There are excellent examples of these. Engagement does not happen outside the university, it happens in created unifying spaces that explore the creation co-development of knowledge, the innovation of solutions and as laboratories for the deepening of participatory democracy. The idea is always that this is not about the university being an agent in the community but rather as a partner in agency. As pointed out earlier, the recent turmoil experienced by South African universities demonstrated a significant legitimacy gap that has opened up between higher education and its publics. The creation of such dynamic interfaces whether through an anchor institutions paradigm (Maurrasse, - this volume) or another, opens up the way for the reconstruction of creative relationships on the one hand and the adoption of integrated cross-disciplinary engagements on the other. One might say that the real world is not so kind to divide itself along disciplinary lines.

Some final thoughts

The deepening of South Africa's adolescent democracy, which is both exciting and sometimes badly behaved, depends on the development of a new generations of civically-engaged intellectuals and servant leaders. Universities are at the centre of creating new cohorts of such individuals through the construction of theory-praxis nexuses that provide students with the opportunity to engage. These nexuses also provide the opportunity for organic leaders to emerge in the communities and civil society structures involved in such engagements.

The key issue it seems is for universities (both as institutions and as a sector) to engage in a process of deliberate design to facilitate the issue of engagement. This has the potential to be transformative in the sense that it may give rise to structures at our institutions which may contribute to the reshaping of the boundaries between universities and their publics, between elements of institutional structures, disciplinary structures and so on. The key issue here is that design plays an important role in determining the nature of engagements between universities and their publics. This cannot be left to chance.

References

Bawa, A.C. 2007. Rethinking the Place of Community-Based Engagement at Universities in *Higher Education and Civic Engagement: International Perspectives*. Edited by Lorraine McIlrath and Iain Mac Labhrainn. Ashgate Publishing Limited 2007, Aldershot/UK. (ISBN 13: 978-0-7546-4889-5)

Bawa, A.C. 2019a. South Africa's Higher Education System in Crisis ... in a State in Crisis. Social Research. Spring 2019. Forthcoming.

Bawa, A.C. 2019b. The Knowledge Project of South Africa's Universities: Breaking Through Isolation by Turning Inwards, Lessons from the Past. In *Transforming Ivory Tower to Ebony Tower*, edited by A. Adebajo, S. Motala and T. Oluwaseun; forthcoming.

CHE 2007. Review of Higher Education in South Africa: Selected Themes. Pretoria. https://www.che.ac.za/sites/default/files/publications/Review_HE_SA_2007_Complete_0.pdf, accessed January 29, 2019.

CHE 2019. https://www.che.ac.za/about/overview_and_mandate/mandate. Accessed January 27, 2019.

de La Rey, C. 2008. Proceedings of the CHE/NRF Workshop on Community Engagement. 22 August 2008, Pretoria.

Lange, L. 2008. Proceedings of the CHE/NRF Workshop on Community Engagement. 22 August 2008, Pretoria.

Gibbons, M., Limoges, C., Nowotny, H., Schwartzman, S., Scott, P., Trow, M. (1994) *The New Production of Knowledge; The Dynamics of Science and Research in Contemporary Societies*. London: Sage Publications.

Hall, M. 2010. Community engagement in South African higher education. Kagisano No. 6. January 2010. CHE, Pretoria.

Higher Education Act 101 of 1997. Pretoria: Department of Education

Kraak, A. (2000) Changing Modes: New Knowledge Production and its Implications for Higher Education in South Africa. Pretoria: Human Sciences Research Council

Liebowitz, B. (2017): 'Cognitive justice and the higher education curriculum' in 'Curriculum stasis, funding and the 'decolonial turn' in universities: Inclusion and exclusion in higher education in South Africa', ed. Jonathan Jansen and Shireen Motala, Journal of Education Number 68, 2017.

Maurrasse, D. (this volume): "What is an Anchor Institution and Why?"

National Advisory Council on Innovation 2017. http://www.naci.org.za/index.php/the-south-african-national-system-of-innovation-structures-policies-and-performance/. Accessed January 27,2019

National Research Foundation 2016. Community Engagement Funding Instrument.

https://www.nrf.ac.za/sites/default/files/documents/CE%20FrameworkDocume nt_2017_Final.pd, accessed January 29, 2019.f

Research England 2019. Knowledge Exchange Framework. https://re.ukri.org/knowledge-exchange/knowledge-exchange-framework/

SciSTIP 2017. SciSTIP 2016 Annual Report. http://www0.sun.ac.za/scistip/wp-content/uploads/2018/03/SciSTIP-2016-Annual-Report.pdf

Transform 2018. Transform No. 2 2017_Online.pdf

THE WAY FORWARD

CHAPTER 13
THE WAY FORWARD

Sjur Bergan, Ira Harkavy, Ronaldo Munck

Introduction

In the preceding pages we have covered much ground in terms of developing a better understanding of The Local Mission of Higher Education from the perspective of university leaders. Many issues were raised that concern both Europe and countries further afield. We show the important local engagement that the higher education institutions already carry out and the need for it to continue and, indeed, expand. It is impossible to summarize here the rich tapestry of the chapters in this book but a few 'take away' points could be the following:

- Higher education institutions need to be anchored or embedded in their local communities;
- Knowledge transfer is a two - way process between the higher education institution and the community;
- Engaging with the local is not incompatible with global engagement, on the contrary;
- We support free speech and also dialogue including inter-cultural dialogue. Dialogue needs to be conducted within and between communities, hence also in local frameworks;
- Higher education needs to support all forms of democracy including the democratization of knowledge, education, and understanding of the world around us;
- We need to respect the diversity of higher education and cannot put forward a 'one size fits all' democratic engagement mission;
- As science, knowledge and even facts are brought into question we need to reaffirm the European values of the Enlightenment as the best way to keep the democratic mission on track.

Theoretical and political context

Before we turn to making some suggestions on 'the way forward' we will seek to clarify a number of the underlying theoretical and political assumptions we all often make when thinking of these issues.

We propose three broad generic questions to set the framework for the way forward:

1. What do we mean by 'local' and how does it function in the era of globalization?
2. What do we mean by 'politics' in the context of higher education and its supposedly traditional 'non-political' role?
3. What might the mission of higher education look like in the global, so-called 'post truth' and 'alternative facts' era we live in?

Most universities now think of themselves as global as much as local or national players. In the era of globalization who would restrict themselves to a purely 'local' role which might be seen as lower down the traditional prestige ranking of what is known as the politics of scale? There is a common tendency to portray the global as 'outside' and the local community as somehow 'inside'. In this caricatured view, 'outside' is the restless movement of finance and people, 'inside' it is a traditional place- based, static community. The first is seen as governed by the new universal, instantaneous, virtual time, the second by the fragmented, nature-bound clock of everyday life. But in practice the scales of human activity are much more inter-linked and the local and the global cannot be seen as separate spheres of social life. That is why we saw the business world in Japan adopt the term 'glocal' at the turn of century (Roudometof 2016). It signals the intrinsic interconnectedness of the local and the global and our need to understand the dual process whereby the local is constantly globalized (think shopping patterns) and the global is constantly localized (think the local branding of global brands). There is no meaningful rationale for establishing a hierarchy between the scales of human activity ranging from the household, to the local community, the sub regional, the national, the supra regional and the global.

What does this conceptual clarification mean for the policy and practice of higher education? Much of our current discourse is based precisely on such a hierarchy of scales: the rankings are global but the 'community stuff' is seen as local. In reality, the aspirations of higher education may be simultaneously global, national, and local. Many higher education institutions will combine all three and see themselves as global, national, and local actors all at the same time. This is generally the case in the United States, at least rhetorically. These institutions, as discussed in previous chapters, often see local engagement as a powerful and effective means for advancing scholarly contributions and promoting institutional standing, nationally as well as globally.

Maybe we can take a further step and reconceptualize our categories to make them more adequate for an age of complexity and fit for purpose in terms of social transformation. For example, we may need to rethink what the regional means in general, standing as it does between the local and the global. This would be important for the development of any higher education institution in the European space in particular. Does the 'national' still mean the same as it did 50 years ago now that it is subject to the forces of globalization but also, in some countries at least, to forces that would emphasize sub-national levels and identities? And what does "regional" mean in terms of a policy orientation dominated by the national level or scale? The regional role of higher education is perhaps more emphasized in the US than in Europe, though there is a growing interest there too (see Chatterton and Goddard 2000). While the term may most often be used to indicate a part of a country, such as the Midwest in the United States or northern Norway[1], or the Moldovan region of Romania[2], at least two other usages are also current. One is a variation on the subnational, but in the sense of a formal administrative entity rather than an informal term to designate a part of a country. One example is the French Région, the number of which was recently reduced from 22 to 13. Another sense, however, is broader and designates a part of the world, such as Europe, North America, or Asia. UNESCO, for example, uses the term in this sense, so that Europe and North America are UNESCO regions, as is Asia and the Pacific. In this book, however, when we have

---

[1] Nord-Norge, which consists of three administrative districts, two of which may be merged depending on the outcome of discussions that are still on-going at the time of writing.

[2] Not to be confused with the Republic of Moldova

referred to "region" or "regional", it has been in the first sense of the term: a part of the country, but not necessarily a formal administrative entity.

Is it possible to imagine a broader European level engaged higher education system that responds to local social need and global challenges? Do the existing structures of funding and policy development suffice to drive this mission?

The second question we need to address is what we mean by 'politics' in the context of higher education. On some US campuses there are calls to allow violent[3] far-right demonstrators on to university grounds on the basis of an (unlimited) right to free speech. In parts of Europe any moves by higher education leaders to protect democratic rights are met by calls that they should not involve themselves in politics (see Deeks 2018). "Politics" is often equated with "party politics". However, this is a very restricted understanding of politics. For sure, there has been resistance in higher education to being dragged into partisan or party politics and for good reason, insofar as the pursuit of knowledge should be an open enterprise. But many movements for emancipation (and of course some opposed to it) have found support in and have emerged from the university. Indeed, they have often helped reinvent political practice and the very meaning of politics (think of feminism for example). We might usefully refer here to Isabelle Stengers (2010) for whom a politics that is not attached to a cosmos/universe is at best debatable, but a cosmos detached from politics is simply irrelevant. That is to say, politics without principles is a dubious proposition but also a world-view without a politics makes it irrelevant in practice.

In terms of our third question - What might the mission of higher education look like in the global, so-called 'post truth' era we live in? - we would argue that the purpose of knowledge itself may well be the continuous betterment of the human condition, which, of course, must involve a values-based conception of what a good community, society, and world might be (see Benson, Harkavy et al. 2017). The university is a space for the development of new knowledge and new principles of human purpose, which often appropriately result in the emergence of

---

[3] Understood as demonstrations that lead to violence directly or that advocates or incites the use of violence.

new imaginaries for emancipation and social change in general. If that is deemed to be politics so be it perhaps.

In a globalized academic world there is a danger that the needs of the market will over-ride all other criteria for success in the realm of higher education. The notion of education as a public good and perhaps also as a public responsibility (Bologna Process 2001, 2003) disappears from view and knowledge becomes purely instrumental. 'Going global' may seem an obvious response to the era of globalization we live in. But it can be a very parochial affair if it simply reproduces one particular model of higher education on a larger canvas. To be global is not the same as to be universal. The latter would drive us towards greater concern with the multidimensionality of contemporary higher education and the pressing need for a greater understanding of multiculturalism. We need to think imaginatively about the location of our institutions and how we can both support our localities and also therefore help ourselves to become more relevant to our societies in all their complexity, problems and prospects. The local mission is not less important than the global and really the two cannot be separated insofar as globalization depends on of localization at the same time. Indeed, we could argue, with Dewey, that democracy must begin at home as it were, in the community (Boydston 1981: 368). As the various contributions to this book show, local democracy is crucial for a genuine participatory democracy.

Finally, we turn to the implications of these points for the mission of higher education, in Europe in particular. Many voices have opposed the strangely named 'post truth' politics and populism – mostly, but not uniquely right wing - now on the ascendancy in many countries. We will likely find that Brexit is a precursor of a new wave of the politics of division and discord now developing to meet the admitted failures of the post-Cold War settlement. It is part of the mission of higher education to generate and gain consensus in society for values we might all share centred on the crucial gains of democracy. In the case of the Council of Europe, these include the values encoded in the European Convention of Human Rights[4]. The Council's White Paper on intercultural dialogue states unequivocally: "The democratic values underpinning the Council of Europe are universal; they are not

[4] For an overview, see https://www.echr.coe.int/Pages/home.aspx?p=basictext s&c, accessed January 28, 2019.

distinctively European" (Council of Europe 2008: 14). The US Declaration of Independence is also rooted in universal values: "We hold these truths to be self-evident, that all men are created equal, that they are endowed by their Creator with certain unalienable Rights, that among these are Life, Liberty and the pursuit of Happiness"[5]. Regardless of one's position on the universality of values or the epistemology of knowledge, these shared values, such as democracy, human rights, and the rule of law should, we argue, undergird the work of the contemporary university. Given its purpose and privileged position as a producer and disseminator of knowledge, the university should aim to be the bearer of universal values. It must, however, engage with society and in particular the local society it is embedded in if it is to realize that goal.

While defending the gains of the enlightenment against all manifestations of irrationalism, we might also with Rorty understand that it is our imagination that helps us extend our sensibilities and our understanding of others. Imagination is one of the best tools we have available and the university needs to be its natural home. It is not linear logic on its own that will resolve the problems of the unequal, conflictual and complex world we live in. We need to open the doors of perception more, not least to develop more empathy and better understanding of others. Academic knowledge alone will not enable us to solve society's problems and build a better life for all, it needs to be engaged with society. Community voice (and knowledge and reason) needs to be involved from the stage of problem identification through problem solution and to implementation. Democratic research and knowledge production may well be a *sine qua non* for genuine intellectual, societal, and global progress. That represents a joining together of the expertise, reason, imagination, and knowledge of the local community and the academy. We thus need to engage more and listen more to our local communities and learn from the wisdom of practice. Only that way will the university be able to rise to the occasion and help lead the fight against unreason and authoritarian populism.

We now return to the promised theme of The Way Forward. We are not seeking to chart a firm path forward at this point; we believe that

---

[5] See http://www.ushistory.org/declaration/document/, accessed January 28, 2019.

will need a broader discussion and debate to make it a more collective shared endeavour. What we propose for now are a number of key questions that we consider need to be asked and answered:

- How can we better embed our higher education institutions within our local communities to build and sustain democracy?
- How can we promote knowledge transfer in a way that benefits and learns from society?
- Can we better tie in the global and the local engagement missions of our higher education institutions?
- Can we make compatible the demand for freedom of speech on our campuses with our duty to defend the rights of our multi-cultural staff and student bodies?
- How can higher education institutions gear up for the growing need to defend and promote democracy in all its facets, including the democratization of knowledge?
- Can we develop a model for local engagement that recognizes the sheer diversity of higher education institutions in terms of size, orientation and mission?
- What form of cooperation will best provide a stable European platform for furthering the local mission of higher education and that will eventually gather institutions of different profiles and ambitions?
- More generally, can there be a specifically European contribution to the defence of democracy based on the shared values of the Enlightenment?

References

Benson, L, Harkavy, I et al (2017) *Knowledge for Social Change. Bacon, Dewey, and the Revolutionary Transformation of Research Universities in the Twenty-First Century*. Philadelpia PA.

Bologna Process (2001): "Towards the European Higher Education Area". Communiqué of the meeting of European Ministers in charge of Higher Education in Prague on May 19th 2001, available at http://www.ehea.info/media.ehea.info/file/2001_Prague/44/2/2001_Prague_Co mmunique_English_553442.pdf, accessed January 28, 2019

Bologna Process (2003): "Realising the European Higher Education Area", Communiqué of the Conference of Ministers responsible for Higher Education in Berlin on 19 September 2003, available at http://www.ehea.info/media.ehea.info/file/2003_Berlin/28/4/2003_Berlin_Comm unique_English_577284.pdf, accessed January 28, 2019

Boydston JA (ed.) (1981): *The Later Works of John Dewey, 1925–1953, vol. 2.* Carbondale: Southern Illinois University; digitally reproduced in Larry Hickman, L. (ed.) (1996): *The Collected Works of John Dewey, 1882–1953: The Electronic Edition.* Charlottesville, VA: InteLex Corporation.

Chatterton P, Goddard JB (2000) 'The response of higher education institutions to regional needs'. European Journal of Education, 35(4), 475-496.

Council of Europe (2008): White Paper on Intercultural Dialogue "Living Together As Equals in Dignity", available at https://www.coe.int/t/dg4 /intercultural/source/white%20paper_final_revised_en.pdf, accessed January 28, 2019

Deeks, A (2018) 'Academic freedom, freedom of expression and the role of university leadership' in S. Bergan and I. Harkavy (ed.) *Higher Education for Diversity, Social Inclusion and Community. A democratic imperative.* Strasbourg: Council of Europe Higher Education Series. No. 22.

Rorty, R. (2000) Philosophy and Social Hope. Penguin.

Roudometof, Victor (2016). *Glocalization: A Critical Introduction* (New York: Routledge).

Stengers, I. (2010) *Cosmopolitics I.* Minnesota University Press.

CONTRIBUTORS

Editors

Sjur Bergan

Sjur Bergan is Head of the Education Department of the Council of Europe and leads its project on Competences for Democratic Culture. He was a member of the editorial group for the Council of Europe's White Paper on Intercultural Dialogue and a main author of the Lisbon Recognition Convention as well as of recommendations on the public responsibility for higher education; academic freedom and institutional autonomy; and ensuring quality education. He represents the Council of Europe in the Bologna Follow-Up Group, and he chaired three successive working groups on structural reform from 2007 to 2015. Bergan is series editor of the Council of Europe Higher Education Series and the author of Qualifications: introduction to a concept and Not by Bread Alone as well as of numerous book chapters and articles on education and higher education policy. He was also one of the editors of the Raabe handbook on Leadership and governance in higher education as well as of most books in the Higher Education Series, most recently Higher education for diversity, social inclusion and community – A democratic imperative (2018, with Ira Harkavy)

Ira Harkavy

Ira Harkavy is Associate Vice President and Founding Director of the Barbara and Edward Netter Center for Community Partnerships at the University of Pennsylvania. A historian with extensive experience working with schools and neighbourhood organizations in Penn's local community of West Philadelphia, Harkavy teaches in the departments of history, urban studies, Africana studies and in the Graduate School of Education. Harkavy is Chair of the Steering Committee of the International Consortium for Higher Education, Civic Responsibility and Democracy, and Chair of the Anchor Institutions Task Force. Harkavy has written and lectured widely on the history and current practice of urban university-community-school partnerships and the democratic and civic missions of higher education. Among his most recent books are Knowledge for Social Change: Bacon, Dewey, and the Revolutionary Transformation of Research Universities in the Twenty First Century (2017, co-authored with Lee Benson, John Puckett,

Matthew Hartley, Rita A. Hodges, Francis E. Johnston, and Joann Weeks), and Higher Education for Diversity, Social Inclusion and Community – A Democratic Imperative (2018, co-edited with Sjur Bergan).

Ronaldo Munck

Ronaldo Munck is Head of Civic Engagement at Dublin City University where he has developed the 'third mission' of engaging teaching and research with the needs of the community. He was founding chair of Campus Engage, the Irish national platform for civic and community engagement. He is co-editor of Higher Education and Civic Engagement: Comparative Perspectives (Palgrave 2012) and Higher Education and Community Based Learning: Creating a Global Vision (Palgrave 2014). He is a Professor of Political Sociology with visiting appointments at the University of Liverpool and St. Mary's University, Nova Scotia. He has written widely on international development issues and on the impact of globalization on work. His recent work includes Rethinking Latin America: Development, Hegemony and Social Transformation (Palgrave 2014) and Rethinking Global Labour: After Neoliberalism (Agenda Publishing 2018). He is on the editorial board of international journals such as Globalizations, Global Social Policy, Global Discourse, Labor History, Global Labour, Labour, Capital and Society, Latin American Perspectives, Review: Fernand Braudel Center and the Canadian Journal of Development Studies. Professor Munck was Irish anchor and a lead author for the influential report by the International Panel on Social Progress chaired by Amartya Sen on alternative futures for global democratic development.

Authors

Ahmed Bawa

Ahmed Bawa is the CEO of Universities South Africa. Until recently he was Vice-Chancellor and Principal of Durban University of Technology. He also served as Deputy Vice-Chancellor of the University of KwaZulu-Natal. He was faculty member in the Department of Physics and Astronomy at Hunter College, City University of New York and a member of the doctoral faculty at the Graduate Center, CUNY. As Program Officer for Higher Education with the Ford Foundation he led the Foundation's African Higher

Education Initiative. He has worked in South Africa, Namibia, Kenya, Tanzania, Uganda, Nigeria, Ghana, Egypt and Palestine. He serves on a number of national and international advisory boards.

Ahmed Bawa holds a Ph.D. in Theoretical Physics from the University of Durham, in the UK. He has published in the areas of high-energy physics; nuclear physics; higher education and society; and science and society.

Tomáš Fliegel

Tomáš Fliegl currently works for the Ministry of Education, Youth and Sports of the Czech Republic as Head of the Strategy Unit in the Higher Education Department. He graduated in Economic Policy and Sociology from Masaryk University (bachelor) and Public and Social Policy from the Charles University (master). In 2013 - 2014 he worked as an analyst and participated in the preparation of the Framework for the Development of Higher Education Institutions until 2020. Since 2014, he has been working at the Department of Higher Education at the Ministry. His research interest is the impact of fees for excessive study duration on time to degree on universities, and he is a co-author of the first Czech publication on higher education drop-out.

Pam Fredman

Pam Fredman is the President of the International Association of Universities (IAU), a membership-based organization created under the auspices of UNESCO in 1950 serving the global higher education community. Her academic background is Professor in Neurochemistry at the University of Gothenburg. She has over the years been active in a large number of scientific and scholarly contexts. During the years 2006-2017, Pam Fredman was the Rector of the University of Gothenburg after being the Head of department of Neurochemistry and the Dean of the Faculty of Health Sciences. Pam Fredman was chair of the SUHF (Swedish Association of Universities and Colleges) and participated in political initiatives and policy development in Sweden but also at Nordic and EU level. She is the government-appointed chair of "The commission of Inquiry on Governance and Resources" to suggest a new model for the steering of and resource allocation to higher education institutions in Sweden,

Tony Gallagher

Tony Gallagher is a Professor of Education at Queen's University Belfast. Currently he is the Acting Faculty Dean of Research for Arts, Humanities and Social Sciences and his previous roles at Queen's have included Pro Vice Chancellor for Academic Planning, Staffing and External Affairs, and Head of the School of Education. His main research interests include the role of education in divided societies, the civic and democratic role of higher education, and the role of social networks on school collaboration. He is a member of the Council of Europe CDPPE sub-group on higher education policy and has served on a number of Council working groups. He is a Deputy Board member of the European Wergeland Centre, Norway, and a Board member for the Maze Long Kesh Development Corporation in Northern Ireland. He is currently researching the role of school collaboration in Northern Ireland, Israel, Los Angeles and Lebanon.

Steinunn Géstsdóttir

Steinunn Géstsdóttir is Pro-rector of Academic Affairs and Development at the University of Iceland and a Professor of Child Development at the Faculty of Psychology. She graduated with a BA in Psychology from the University of Iceland in 1996, an MA in Psychology from the University of Boston in 2001, and a PhD in Developmental Psychology from Tufts University in 2005.

Steinunn Géstsdóttir started her academic career at the University of Education in Iceland, and since 2009 she has held a position at the Faculty of Psychology at the University of Iceland. In 2015 she became a full professor and from 2016 she has also held the position of Pro-Rector for Academic Affairs and Development. In her research, Steinunn has primarily focused on self-regulation among children and youth and its role in positive development. Dr. Gestsdottir has been involved in policy making relating to higher education and reserach within the University of Iceland and at national level. She leads the implementation of the Strategy of the University of Iceland, is a member of the Icelandic Science and Technology Policy Council, and was a board member of the Icelandic Research Fund and the Icelandic Student Innovation Fund.

Stanisław Kistryn

Professor Stanisław Kistryn, a physicist, specialized in nuclear physics and is a co-author of more than 180 scientific papers. He is the current President of the European Few-Body Research Committee. Since 2012, he has been Vice-Rector for research and structural funds at the Jagiellonian University in Kraków. He has participated as a member in a number of committees and expert groups associated with the Polish Ministry of Science and Higher Education. He has been designated as one of a few consultants for the preparation of the new law on science and higher education. Since 2011, he has been concerned with evaluating research projects within the NuPNET programme for Ministry of Science and Innovation of Spain. Professor Kistryn represents the Jagiellonian University in several international university networks EUA, Coimbra Group, the Guild of European Research Intensive Universities (where he served as a first term Board Member/Treasurer), and in the newly established "European University Alliance" UNA EUROPA.

Liviu Matei

Liviu Matei is the Provost of the Central European University (CEU) and a Professor of Higher Education Policy at the CEU's School of Public Policy. He directs the Yehuda Elkana Center for Higher Education. A higher education policy scholar and practitioner with teaching, research and consulting experience in Europe, Asia and North America, he has coordinated or taken part in major policy projects in higher education at the institutional, national, regional and international level in these regions. He is a member of the Board of Trustees of the American University of Central Asia and serves on the editorial boards of the European Journal of Higher Education and the Internationalization of Higher Education Journal.

David Maurrasse

David Maurrasse is the Founder and President of Marga Incorporated, a consulting firm founded in 2000 providing strategic advice and research to philanthropic initiatives and community partnerships. Marga coordinates the Anchor Institutions Task Force – an action-oriented learning community with over 900 members, promoting the role of enduring organizations in community and economic development, for which Dr. Maurrasse serves as Director. Marga also coordinates the Race and Equity in Philanthropy Group (REPG), which strengthens foundations' policies and practices on racial equity, diversity, and inclusion. Maurrasse is a Senior Fellow at the New World Foundation.

Since 2000, David Maurrasse has been affiliated with Columbia University, where he currently serves as Research Scholar and Adjunct Associate Professor at the School of International and Public Affairs. Dr. Maurrasse was an Assistant Professor at Yale University, and a Senior Program Advisor at the Rockefeller Foundation. Dr. Maurrasse has published numerous books, including Strategic Public Private Partnerships: Innovation and Development (2013), Listening to Harlem (2006), A Future for Everyone: Innovative Social Responsibility and Community Partnerships (2004), Beyond the Campus: How Colleges and Universities Form Partnerships with Their Communities (2001). His most recent book project is entitled Philanthropy and Society (2019).

Joanna Ozarowska

Joanna Ozarowska is the Manager of DCU in the Community - a community outreach, adult education and community-based learning centre at Dublin City University. She is currently pursuing a Doctorate in Education (D.Ed.) programme at the Department of Adult and Community Education, Maynooth University, and her research interests focus on the civic and social mission of higher education. Her professional practice crosses over the areas of civic engagement, adult education, widening access and inclusion in higher education, and student volunteering. She has also been involved at steering and advisory committee level in local community and non-governmental organizations. Ozarowska is a member of Campus Engage Ireland and co-led the development of the national online student volunteering platform studentvolunteer.ie, in addition to serving as DCU representative on the Campus Engage Community-Based Learning Working Group. She is currently a joint lead on the Irish Aid funded Vietnam-Ireland Bilateral Education Exchange project that focuses on developing and promoting community-based learning practices for STEM subjects in Vietnam.

Spyros Syropoulos

Spyros Syropoulos is Professor of Classics at the Department of Mediterranean Studies of the University of the Aegean, in Rhodes and Secretary General of the Greek Rectors' Council. He was Vice Rector of International Relations, Student Affairs and Alumni of the University of the Aegean between 2014 and 2018. Spŷros Syropoulos is director of the Master's Course Theater as a Social and Political Institution in the Mediterranean during Antiquity (University of the Aegean) as well as of the summer school "Europe as a Common" (Syros, Greece, Sept. 2018). He is a member of the Council of Monuments and Antiquities in Rhodes (branch of the National Archaeological Council) and a former member of the council of the International Center of Writers and Translators in Rhodes (2003-2011, Vice President between 2006-2011). He has participated in several historical documentaries for television (BBC2, History Channel, TRT etc) and is the author of five books and many articles related to his professional expertise.

Barbora Vokšická

Barbora Vokšická is currently a student in the teacher training programme for primary schools as well as in political science and public policy at the Charles University. Her professional interest is the quality of teacher training programmes and innovative teaching approaches. She worked as an intern for the Higher Education Department of the Ministry of Education, Youth and Sports of the Czech Republic during autumn 2018.

Joann Weeks

Joann Weeks is an associate director of the University of Pennsylvania's Netter Center for Community Partnerships, focusing on its regional, national and international programmes. She directs the national adaptation of the Netter Center's university-assisted community school programme as well as its training and technical assistance activities, including the university-assisted community schools network. She supervises the staff of the Philadelphia Higher Education Network for Neighborhood Development (PHENND), a consortium of nearly 30 institutions of higher education in the Philadelphia region. Weeks works closely with the Anchor Institutions Task Force leadership. She is Executive Secretary for the International Consortium for Higher Education, Civic Responsibility and Democracy, which works in

151

collaboration with the Council of Europe and the Organization of American States. Ms. Weeks has worked closely with the national Coalition for Community Schools since its inception in 1997 and is a member of its Community School Leaders Network and Steering Committee. Ms. Weeks is associate editor of Penn's Universities and Community Schools journal.

Radka Wildová

Radka Wildová was Dean of the Faculty of Education of Charles University from 2009 to 2016 and has been Vice-Rector for Education since 2016. She is active in the Association of the Deans of Pedagogical Faculties of the Czech Republic and is a member of the team of advisors to the Minister for Education, Youth and Sports. Her chief professional interests are the issues of initial literacy, the didactics of primary education, professional preparation of educational workers and educational policy. She is the author of several dozen publications in journals and anthologies in both the Czech Republic and abroad and also of several monographs, the most important of which include Reading Literacy and the Support of its Development in School. Her books for teaching initial literacy are known to the wider pedagogical public. She is a member of the Scientific Councils of several foreign universities and associations (e.g. the International Reading Association) and regularly lectures at universities abroad. She is a delegate to the Steering Committee for Education Policy and Practice of the Council of Europe and a member of its sub-group on higher education policy.

Also Available from Glasnevin Publishing

Politics, Participation & Power
Edited by Deiric O'Broin and Mary
Murphy
ISBN-13: 978-1-908689-19-1

The Nuts and Bolts of Innovation
Edited by David Jacobson
ISBN-13: 978-1908689-25-2

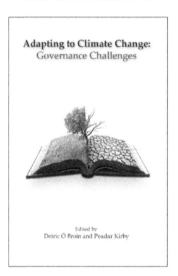

Adapting to Climate Change
Edited by Deiric O'Broin and Peadar Kirby
ISBN-13: 978-1908689-30-6

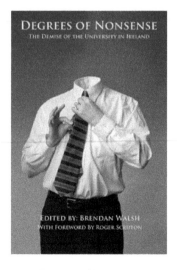

Degrees of Nonsense
Edited by Brendan Walsh
ISBN-13: 978-1-9086891-02-3

Lightning Source UK Ltd.
Milton Keynes UK
UKHW041918140519
342652UK00002B/171/P

9 781908 689368